201 Healthy Smoothies & Juices for Kids

Fresh, Wholesome, No-Sugar-Added Drinks Your Child Will Love

AMY ROSKELLEY
Founder of SuperHealthyKids.com
with **NICOLE CORMIER, RD, LDN**

Aadamsmedia

Avon, Massachusetts

Published by
Adams Media, a division of F+W Media, Inc.
57 Littlefield Street, Avon, MA 02322. U.S.A.
www.adamsmedia.com

Contains material adapted and abridged from *The Everything® Juicing Book*, by Carole Jacobs and Chef
Patrice Johnson with Nicole Cormier, RD, copyright © 2010 by F+W Media, Inc., ISBN 10: 1-4405-0326-5, ISBN
13: 978-1-4405-0326-9; and *The Everything® Green Smoothies Book*, by Britt Brandon with Lorena Novak Bull,
RD, copyright © 2011 by F+W Media, Inc., ISBN 10: 1-4405-2564-1, ISBN 13: 978-1-4405-2564-3.

ISBN 10: 1-4405-3364-4
ISBN 13: 978-1-4405-3364-8
eISBN 10: 1-4405-3612-0
eISBN 13: 978-1-4405-3612-0

Printed in the United States of America.

10 9 8 7 6 5 4 3 2 1

Library of Congress Cataloging-in-Publication Data
Roskelley, Amy.
  201 healthy smoothies and juices for kids / Amy Roskelley, founder of SuperHealthyKids.com.
    pages cm
  Includes bibliographical references and index.
  ISBN 978-1-4405-3364-8 (pbk. : alk. paper) – ISBN 1-4405-3364-4 (pbk. : alk. paper) – ISBN
978-1-4405-3612-0 (ebook) – ISBN 1-4405-3612-0 (ebook)
  1. Smoothies (Beverages) 2. Fruit juices–Health aspects. 3. Vegetable juices–Health aspects.
  4. Children–Nutrition. I. Title. II. Title: Two hundred one healthy smoothies and juices for kids.
  III. Title: Two hundred and one healthy smoothies and juices for kids.
    TX840.B5R67 2012
    641.3'4–dc23
                                            2011050143

This publication is designed to provide accurate and authoritative information with regard to the subject matter
covered. It is sold with the understanding that the publisher is not engaged in rendering legal, accounting, or
other professional advice. If legal advice or other expert assistance is required, the services of a competent
professional person should be sought.
                    —From a *Declaration of Principles* jointly adopted by a Committee of the
                    American Bar Association and a Committee of Publishers and Associations

This book is intended as general information only, and should not be used to diagnose or treat any health
condition. In light of the complex, individual, and specific nature of health problems, this book is not intended
to replace professional medical advice. The ideas, procedures, and suggestions in this book are intended to
supplement, not replace, the advice of a trained medical professional. Consult your physician before adopting
any of the suggestions in this book, as well as about any condition that may require diagnosis or medical
attention. The author and publisher disclaim any liability arising directly or indirectly from the use of this book.

Many of the designations used by manufacturers and sellers to distinguish their product are claimed as
trademarks. Where those designations appear in this book and Adams Media was aware of a trademark claim,
the designations have been printed with initial capital letters.

This book is available at quantity discounts for bulk purchases.
For information, please call 1-800-289-0963.

Dedication

This book is dedicated to my family and the amazing online community that has made this book possible.

Acknowledgments

I would like to thank my kids, who lovingly drank their hearts out and drowned themselves in smoothies and juices along with me.

Contents

3 Ready for Anything: Drinks on the Go 86

SMOOTHIES

JUICES

4 Better Snacks for Better Kids: Drinks with a Purpose 133

5 Just for Fun (and Then Some): Drinks for Dessert 182

Introduction

One Sunday afternoon, I had prepared what I thought was a delicious dinner for my family: lasagna, fresh spinach salad, and whole-wheat rolls. My oldest child, who was about four at the time, declared he was full before dinner even started. He told us he had absolutely no room in his stomach for any of the food that was on his plate. Of course, being an enlightened mother in the twenty-first century, and not wanting to feed my child when his hunger cues told him not to eat, I allowed him to visit with us during the meal and not eat a single bite of his dinner. Then we dished up dessert. My son in the most sincere tone informed us that although he was not hungry for dinner, he was definitely hungry for dessert. That was the first of hundreds, if not thousands, of similar conversations between me and my children. They are hesitant to eat what is good for them, going so far as to say they are too full to eat, yet so quick to dive into dessert as if they hadn't eaten all day.

If your family is anything like mine, this story is familiar! Kids have a huge variety of healthy and not-so-healthy food to choose from today. It's easy for them to pick and choose the foods they are "hungry" for. Store shelves are crowded with bright packages of foods, with new ones being added daily. Unfortunately, these attractive foods aren't necessarily good for our children. Many of them are filled with preservatives, artificial ingredients, synthetic dyes, processed sugars, and large amounts of sodium.

We know that our children should consume real foods like whole fruits and vegetables in order to receive vital nutrients without the added sugars and empty calories. Whole fruits and vegetables provide children with the perfect balance of proteins, carbohydrates, essential fats, vitamins, and minerals.

But how can we get them to eat these fruits and vegetables? Our kids may not like the flavors or textures. And in our fast-paced, fast-food world, sometimes we just see fruits and vegetables as too inconvenient. Washing, chopping, preparing, and cooking are sometimes too much of a hassle.

Homemade smoothies and juices are the perfect answer for today's kids. These fruit- and vegetable-based drinks have all the good stuff of fresh fruits and vegetables, minus all the bad stuff of preservatives, synthetic dyes, sugars, and sodium. They can provide kids with essential nutrients in a way they won't complain about. As your kids begin to make a habit of drinking fresh juices and smoothies, you can feel confident that they not only survive the sick season but thrive the whole year. This cookbook is the solution for showing you how to make smoothies and juices your kids will always be hungry for. Instead of refusing fruits and vegetables, they'll be asking for more!

How to Use This Book

This book is your go-to reference for making healthy changes in your children's diet. Whether you are just beginning this journey or have been committed to healthy habits all along, the juice and smoothie recipes in this book will help you on your way.

Customize It!

Each smoothie recipe can be custom-made for the way your kids like it. We almost always add a few ice cubes to our smoothies if we aren't using frozen fruit. The ice gives smoothies a milkshake texture that my kids enjoy. The juice recipes can also be customized. My kids enjoy juice more when I add a touch of water to make it thinner and chill the drink in the fridge for a few minutes so it's super-cold.

How the Book Is Organized

Chapter 1: Helping Kids Become Super Healthy shows you how the juices and smoothies in this book can help your kids become healthier—and stay that way. The recipes themselves are divided into four chapters.

Chapter 2: Morning Sunshine: Drinks to Jump-Start the Day contains smoothies and juices that are perfect for starting the day in the healthiest way possible. The fuel our kids consume after waking up should be full of good carbohydrates to get them going, and the smoothies and juices in this chapter do just that— while keeping out the artificial junk of traditional breakfast cereals. Replacing sugar-laced cereals with a smoothie or fresh juice is best for sending kids to a long day of school. The midmorning sugar crash will go away, and they'll be able to pay attention in class better.

Chapter 3: **Ready for Anything: Drinks on the Go** gives your family recipes for smoothies and juices that are perfect for kids on the move. When your family is busy and you need to grab and go, these are the best recipes for you. These drinks are ideal for heading out to soccer, or even just spending a day on the lake.

Chapter 4: In **Better Snacks for Better Kids: Drinks with a Purpose**, each recipe has a specific feature that will help make kids healthier. From helping quash motion sickness to enhancing memory to strengthening immunity, the recipes in this chapter will boost your kids' health.

Chapter 5: **Just for Fun (and Then Some): Drinks for Dessert** contains all the delicious dessert recipes you can imagine. Birthday parties, celebrations, and after-dinner treats can now be filled with health and wellness instead of sugar and illness. The best part is kids will enjoy these treats as much as, or even more than, traditional dessert foods.

Reading the Recipes

Each recipe is designed to appeal to kids and to be simple for parents to whip up. To make the recipes even more helpful than usual, the recipes feature several bonuses.

Super Sidebars

Each recipe includes a sidebar packed with details about the recipe that will help you in your journey to wellness. You'll find six different types of sidebars:

- **Time Saver Tip.** This type of sidebar gives shortcuts and ideas for saving time and making the recipes as quickly as possible.

- **Nutrition News.** This type of sidebar offers information on how certain ingredients in the smoothies and juices will help your children stay healthy.

- **DIY.** This type of sidebar offers do-it-yourself ideas for making the most of the juices and smoothies in this book and to encourage your children to eat healthfully.

- **Picky Eater.** This type of sidebar gives ideas and techniques for helping picky eaters learn to love their fruits and veggies.

- **Green Tip.** This type of sidebar gives you choices for being as environmentally conscious as possible when making and serving these juices and smoothies.

- **Make It Fun.** This type of sidebar shows how you can make eating healthfully fun for kids, instead of a drudgery or chore.

Reading the Icons

Throughout the book, each recipe also includes icons that show that recipe's special feature. Look for recipes that contain superfoods, those that are great to make in big batches, drinks that should be consumed fresh, drinks that you can store for later, drinks for the whole family, drinks that are great for athletes, drinks that are great for immunity, and those that include dairy.

MEANING OF THE ICONS			
ICON	**MEANING**	**ICON**	**MEANING**
	Superfood		Whole family enjoys
	Big batches		Especially good for athletes
	Drink fresh		Immune support
	Keeps well		Includes dairy

Nutritional Analysis

The recipes in this book include full nutrition data. You'll see a listing that looks like this:

CALORIES	FAT	PROTEIN	SODIUM	CARBOHYDRATES	SUGARS	FIBER
74	0 grams	1 gram	1 milligram	19 grams	16 grams	2 grams

That means that particular recipe has 74 calories per serving, no grams of fat, 1 gram of protein, 1 milligram of sodium, 19 grams of carbohydrates, 16 grams of sugars, and 2 grams of fiber.

Recommended Dietary Allowance

To know how these recipes fit into a healthy eating plan for your children, check out the Mayo Clinic's nutritional charts by age and gender. It will help you determine the appropriate amount of these nutrients for your child depending on his or her age: *www.mayoclinic.com/health/nutrition-for-kids/NU00606*

1

Helping Kids Become Super Healthy

Like most parents, you want what's best for your children, but you're pressed for time, money, or energy—or all three! So you may end up giving your kids less-than-perfect meals as a result. Still, you want to do better—you're just not sure how. This cookbook is the answer! You'll learn how to use juices and smoothies to improve your children's health and nutrition, even if you are low on time, money, and energy! Ensuring good nutrition doesn't have to be time-consuming, expensive, or hard.

Let's start by looking at the facts—what your kids *should* be eating.

Dietary Recommendations: the American Academy of Pediatrics

According to the American Academy of Pediatrics (AAP), children ages two to eight should eat:

- 1–1½ cups fruits per day

- 1½–2 cups of vegetables per day

- 3–5 ounces of grains

- 2–4 ounces of beans or meats

- 2 cups of milk

- 3–4 teaspoons of oil

That seems simple enough on the surface, but you know that getting that much fruit and veggies into your children can be a challenge. Serve a kid a cup of boiled green beans and you're probably not going to have much luck getting it down the hatch without a lot of stress and frustration on both sides. That's why juices and smoothies are such a blessing! It's a lot easier to convince your child to down a delicious smoothie.

The AAP recommendations allow for half of the fruit servings to be in the form of fruit juices (not fruit-flavored drinks). Specifically, kids ages one to four could drink 6 ounces of fruit juice per day, and kids over ten can drink up to 12 ounces per day. Infants younger than six months should not consume juices in any form. The AAP further recommends juice should only be offered to a child who can drink from a cup. Juice should never be served to babies or toddlers through a bottle as that tends to promote cavities.

The AAP also recommends juice and fruit-based drinks be part of a meal or snack, rather than sipped throughout the day. This is a great opportunity for teaching kids that fruits and vegetables are part of a balanced meal. When you make the juices and smoothies together, kids also learn where their food and drinks originate, giving them a greater connection to their food.

Your Child's Natural Eating Habits

Kids grow at different rates and sometimes even go through periods where their growth is slowed considerably. During these times, kids naturally eat less and sometimes significantly decrease the amount of food and calories they are comfortable eating each day. It's not necessary to force your kids to eat all the food recommended by the AAP. These guidelines can help you plan meals for your children, shop for food to stock your pantry, or prepare that midday snack for your hungry kids, but don't worry if your kid is eating less than usual. Do, however, make sure that they're not replacing good-for-them food with less-than-desirable options.

Putting Recommendations into Practice

Other organizations have developed guidelines that will help you make good decisions about your children's nutrition. For example, the USDA recommends for children (and adults!) age two and above:

- Half your plate should consist of fruit and vegetables.
- Cut back on foods high in solid fats, added sugars, and salt. This includes most processed foods and baked goods.
- Choose 100 percent fruit juice instead of fruit-flavored drinks.
- Eat a variety of vegetables, especially colorful vegetables.

Using these simple rules of thumb will help you ensure your children are getting adequate nutrition.

The Importance of Good Nutrition

Good nutrition helps children become and stay healthy. It also helps them maintain an appropriate body weight (obesity among children is becoming a serious health problem; according to the Centers for Disease Control and Prevention, nearly 20 percent of children are obese).

Eating fruits and vegetables gives children's bodies the proper nutrients necessary to work as efficiently as possible. Without essential nutrients, phytochemicals, and antioxidants, kids would not have the building blocks necessary to build new bone, muscle, and heart tissue. These nutrients also keep all of their organs functioning properly.

Eating a variety of the recommended amount of fruits and vegetables provides kids with:

- A decreased risk for heart disease, stroke, digestive diseases, and type 2 diabetes.

- An improved and strengthened immune system with the ability to protect and fight against infections. This means fewer sick days for kids.

- An ability to maintain a healthy weight.

- Better vision and healthier skin.

- Healthier gums and teeth.

- A decreased risk for cancers.

- Improved digestion. Fiber is essential for optimal digestion, and it is only available in plant foods.

- More energy to play! Kids who eat well run faster and longer than the kids who are fueled by junk.

- A preference for healthier food. The more fruits and veggies they eat, the more they want to eat, creating the conditions for lifelong good health.

- Better brain function.

- Better sleep.

- Increased longevity.

The Solutions

So, we know that eating more fruits and vegetables will help our children thrive, but it can be a challenge to get kids to consume them! Kids aren't the only ones who struggle with this. Adults also find it hard to consume enough fruits and vegetables. One way they meet this challenge is to blend up smoothies and squeeze fruits and vegetables for their juices. Done well, this can be a delicious way to supplement or even replace meals while getting in the dietary requirements for fruits and vegetables every day. Why not do the same for our children as well? Our kids can enjoy and benefit from this trend just as we do. However, instead of using smoothies and juices for detoxes or weight loss, we can tailor the smoothies and juices we make for our kids to promote good health and good nutrition.

Picky Eaters

Kids who have become accustomed to processed and overly sugary or salty foods are the toughest ones to convert to more nutritious foods. I received an e-mail from a desperate mother, Aileene, a few weeks back. Aileene said, "My kids won't eat anything orange. Actually, they won't eat any fruits and vegetables for that matter. What can I do?" These pleas for help come into my inbox almost daily. When you make the decision to feed your family better, it's frustrating when the kids don't jump right on board. You take the time and spend the money on healthy food to make a positive impact in their lives only for your kids to turn up their noses and declare it "looks too gross" to try.

Fruit and vegetable smoothies are perfect for hiding vegetables for picky eaters. After blending, there is generally no indication which vegetable you have included in their drinks beyond the color. Even the pickiest eaters will be fooled by the smoothies' natural sweetness, not even realizing there could be veggies in their cup. You can include spinach, broccoli, kale, and other bitter greens that kids seldom like when simply served on a plate.

At the end of the day, it takes creative and clever parents to help their kids meet the daily requirements for fruits and vegetables. We work with what we've got and keep trying until something sticks. Blending up and juicing fruits and vegetables can work wonders because it bypasses most kids' "gross factor" radar. Kids are more likely to try a smoothie than a plate of spinach. Kids are more likely to drink a glass of juice than eat a carrot.

Persistence Pays

It's important to keep trying and be persistent to develop good health habits. Whether your children accept your drinks initially or not, don't give up. As you consistently offer fruit- and vegetable-based drinks, your kids will slowly form important habits that they will keep the rest of their lives. You can include fruit and vegetable drinks for mealtimes or for snacks. Drink them yourself to encourage your children to do the same. Incorporating these drinks at mealtime will teach kids it is food and part of your meals. As you enjoy the foods you want your kids to consume, they will want to eat the way you do. Instead of drinking coffee for breakfast and telling them they can't have any, the whole family can drink a nice fresh glass of juice together.

It takes time for children to develop a taste and a love for fruits and vegetables. Exposing your kids to these foods in all their forms is a great way to help them expand their palates. So break out the juicers and the blenders, and give your kids the best start in life possible. Fill them up each day with a glass full of vitamins and minerals rather than sugar and chemicals. They'll be healthier, happier, and better-equipped to take on the day.

Homemade Smoothies

Smoothies have become popular in the last few years as an easy way to consume extra fruits and vegetables. Any combination of fruits and vegetables put together into a blender could be called a smoothie. Preparing these drinks at home is far superior to any smoothies you may get in the grocery store or at restaurant. Those commercially prepared smoothies often contain more sugar than a typical soda pop. One particular orange smoothie at a popular restaurant contains 108 grams of sugar for a 20-ounce cup. This is equivalent to 27 teaspoons of sugar! This smoothie actually has more sugar than an equivalent-sized soda. Children don't need added sugar in their diet from commercially prepared drinks.

Benefits of Homemade Smoothies for Kids

When I asked my twelve-year-old why kids drink smoothies, he responded with, "Cause they're delicious!" In a child's mind, it often is irrelevant whether something is going to be good for them or not. The question, "Does it taste good?" reigns supreme. Kids will eat cake because it tastes good, but they will also eat broccoli if prepared in a way that they think tastes good. Kids who love ice cream milkshakes will love smoothies, too. Smoothies just taste great!

They're also fun for kids to make. My daughter began making a simple smoothie with a bag of frozen tropical fruit mix and milk. That was all she used, and she and her friend loved it.

Smoothies are convenient and portable. Sometimes we have less than five minutes from the moment my son walks in the door after school until we have to leave for soccer practice. I can have a smoothie waiting for him to grab and bring with us on the way. Not only is it refreshing and hydrating, he gets some easy-to-absorb carbs to fuel his practice.

Drinking fruit and vegetable smoothies is the perfect gateway for kids to become familiar with different tastes and flavors of fruits and vegetables. The more variety kids have when they are young, the more likely they are to explore and taste new, healthy foods. It's a way to get them into the habit of increasing their consumption of fruits and veggies while they are young. These habits set them up for a lifetime of healthy eating.

Making smoothies is also a great way to use up any overripe bananas and apples or any vegetable that has lost its crispness. In my house, bananas are always eaten when they are yellow. None of my children will try a green banana, and they all avoid the bananas with even one spec of brown on the peel. When bananas get brown, you can throw them right into the freezer, peel and all, and keep until you are ready to make smoothies with them. It's much quicker and cleaner to make smoothies from overripe bananas than to make banana bread. The produce in your house never has to be wasted again. Instead of the garbage can where fruits go that are past their prime, dump them in a blender instead.

Health Benefits of Smoothies

Smoothies made from whole fruits and vegetables contain all the nutrients origi-nally packaged in that food. When kids drink homemade smoothies, none of the nutrients are lost! Not even the fiber. These fruits and vegetables retain all the good things about them, in an easy-to-consume form.

For decades, scientists have been trying to isolate, study, and package indi-vidual nutrients out of fruits and vegetables. Although well intentioned, they have found isolated nutrients are less effective than the whole foods themselves.

When you take vitamin C out of an orange and put it in a capsule, the results are less than optimal. What supplements fail to replicate is the synergism that occurs when the vitamins are combined with all other parts of the fruit. The vitamins and minerals work together and allow the nutrients to be more easily absorbed by the presence of each other. The impact on blood sugar levels is moderated with the presence of the fiber of the whole foods. Homemade smoothies are perfect for maximum nutrient absorption because the whole fruit and the whole vegetables are present. Keeping the vitamins, minerals, phytochemicals, antioxidants, and fiber intact makes a homemade smoothie a much better alternative to supplements than isolating these nutrients. There is no longer a need to convince your kids to take their vitamins if they are drinking smoothies every day.

Raw fruits and vegetables are rich in enzymes, which assists with all the basic functions in our bodies. Homemade smoothies retain these enzymes, improving children's ability to absorb nutrients, remove toxins, metabolize food, build new cells, and fight infections. The process of cooking fruits and vegetables destroys many of these enzymes. Blending raw fruits and vegetables up into a smoothie, however, keeps these life-giving enzymes intact.

The physical process of blending up fruits and vegetables into a smoothie actually helps break down the food in a way that allows us to absorb the nutrients better. The cells of plant-based food contain the nutrients our bodies need. When we chew our food, we break the cell wall to release the essential vitamins and minerals. We are able to absorb between 15–25 percent of these nutrients when we chew our food. Blending food, however, allows us to absorb up to 95 percent of the nutrients in the plant food.

Homemade smoothies are a great vehicle for fiber for a child. Most kids aren't getting the recommended amount of fiber each day. A low-fiber diet can cause gastrointestinal distress and constipation. Drinking smoothies can help prevent these problems.

Essential Smoothie Ingredients

A smoothie really needs nothing more than some fruits or vegetables, blended up until smooth, to be good. However, there are tons of fresh ingredients you can include to ensure your smoothies are packed with nutrients and flavor.

VEGETABLES

- Beets
- Broccoli
- Carrots
- Celery
- Cucumbers
- Kale
- Peppers
- Potatoes
- Radishes
- Romaine and other leafy greens
- Spinach
- Squash
- String beans
- Swiss chard
- Tomatoes

SPROUTS, NUTS, AND SEEDS

- Alfalfa sprouts
- Almonds
- Peanuts
- Pecans
- Pumpkin seeds
- Sesame seeds
- Soy beans
- Sunflower seeds
- Walnuts

FRUITS

- Apples
- Apricots
- Avocado
- Bananas
- Blackberries
- Blueberries
- Cantaloupe
- Cherries
- Cranberries
- Grapefruit
- Grapes
- Honeydew melon
- Kiwi
- Lemons
- Limes
- Mangoes
- Nectarines
- Oranges
- Papaya
- Peaches
- Pears
- Pineapple
- Plums
- Raspberries
- Strawberries
- Watermelon

LIQUIDS

- Almond milk
- Fruit juices
- Milk
- Rice milk
- Soy milk
- Water
- Yogurt

SWEETENERS

- Agave nectar
- Honey
- Maple syrup

HERBS, SPICES, AND FLAVORINGS

- Garlic
- Ginger
- Mint
- Vanilla

EXTRAS

- Flaxseed or flax oil
- Protein powder
- Tofu
- Wheat germ

Tips and Tricks to Making
Smoothies Kids Will Eat

You've made a delicious-looking, delicious-tasting smoothie, and your kid won't drink it. Now what? Don't throw it down the sink just yet! Get creative, and soon enough they'll be asking for a smoothie every morning.

1 **Make sure they're hungry.** One way to get kids to drink their smoothies when you are first starting out is to make sure they are hungry enough to enjoy it. Food always tastes better when we're hungry. There are many times my kids have come inside after a long day of playing and will eat almost anything that I have prepared. Every new food we introduce to my kids, I give them on an empty stomach. A child who has been grazing all day on graham crackers and cereal is hardly ever tempted by a smoothie.

2 **Keep it familiar.** This is especially important for kids who are uncomfortable trying new things. Make sure there is a familiar ingredient in their smoothie. For a kid who loves strawberries, prepare a strawberry-spinach smoothie. Slowly incorporating new ingredients into their cups is better than surprising them with something totally new and foreign to them.

3 **Freeze it.** Try pouring the smoothie into an ice pop mold and freezing it. Then, when the kids ask for a snack, break out the smoothie pops and let them go to town! We've compared our smoothie pops with commercially frozen ice treats, and our smoothie pops always taste better, and they are better for them.

4 **Keep it smooth.** Smoothies are supposed to be exactly that—smooth! If your child cannot sip her smoothie through a straw, it needs to be either blended longer, or you should look into purchasing a better blender. Two things help me to get my smoothies extra-smooth. One is to add extra liquid to assist the blender in mixing. The second is either to precut my fruits and vegetables into smaller pieces for easier blending, or to slightly defrost frozen fruits or vegetables.

Juicing at Home

A study just published by the Centers for Disease Control and Prevention reported that half of Americans drink sugar-sweetened drinks every day. The drinks included in the study were sodas, fruit drinks, energy drinks, sports drinks, and sweetened bottled water. While the American Heart Association recommends drinking no more than 450 calories of sugary sweetened drinks *per week*, average consumption is at a staggering 300 calories *per day*!

Best Reasons to Juice with Your Kids

Kids drink a lot of juice, some of it with added sugar. Making homemade juice for your kids will ensure they're drinking healthier juices. Plus, you'll save money, they'll get much needed nutrients, they'll be able to take their healthy creations on the road, and it will teach them that the true origin of their food is from plants and not from a box. The daily health habits you'll be able to instill in your kids while they are young are priceless.

SAVE MONEY

You will save money juicing! Many people shy away from juicing because they assume it will be too expensive. This couldn't be further from the truth. Although, ounce for ounce, it may feel like you are paying more for homemade juices, store-bought juices often have unhealthy sugars added. Even 100 percent fruit juices when store-bought generally have more water than they have fruit. When you make your kids' juices at home, you can be sure you are giving them every bit of the fruit and vegetable you have paid for.

What's more, juicing saves money because it gives you another way to use fruits and vegetables instead of letting them go to waste. When fruits and veggies are nearing the end of their shelf life, you can juice and serve. Or, you can freeze the juice in ice cube trays or freezer-safe bags to use another time.

The savings don't have to stop there. Repurposing the pulp after juicing is a way to use up all the parts of your fruits and vegetables without being wasteful. Adding your leftover pulp to pancakes, muffins, sweet breads, or sauces will give your family tons of extra fiber, with no extra costs.

EXTRA NUTRIENTS

In a country where few people eat the recommended requirements for fruits and vegetables, and the most common vegetable consumed is French fries, juicing becomes not only a great way for your kids to meet these requirements but almost a necessity. Children in families who make their own juices are meeting and exceeding those guidelines. Juicing allows kids to consume a concentrated amount of nutrients in a small amount of juice. While it's vital to balance a child's intake of juice with whole foods, juicing can definitely fill a gap.

IT'S EASY

Juicing is so easy, even a child can do it! I remember the day I brought home our first juicer. My kids all wanted to take it out of the box and just start juicing stuff. I was busy, so finally I said, "Oh, go ahead! I don't care." I came into the kitchen a few minutes later, and they each were drinking their own cup of apple juice. It took them a total of five minutes to unpack the box, plug it in, cut an apple, and make juice. Of course they left the cleanup to me, but I was happy they were juicing.

IT'S PORTABLE

Juice boxes haven't become so popular because kids are drinking their juice at the kitchen table—it's because kids are constantly on the go. Whether you are on your way to soccer, sending juice for school lunch, or just hanging out at the swimming pool, you can use homemade juices. Keep your juices cold by using a Thermos or other insulated cup. In our family, when we know we want to bring juice on the road, we'll often freeze the homemade juice and bring it frozen. That way, the juice stays cold until the kids are ready to drink it.

PACKAGING AND PRESERVATIVES

Making your own juice allows you to control what is going into your drinks and what the juice is being served in. Commercial drinks are often full of food additives such as synthetic dyes, artificial flavors, and preservatives. Many kids are sensitive to these dyes and preservatives, and we would never think of adding them to real food. The research is just beginning on the possible harmful effects these preservatives and dyes could have on our kids. The packaging also poses a concern: We don't know yet the effects from the lining of cardboard juice boxes or foil pouches can have on our kids.

The packaging from these drinks fills our landfills with wasteful plastic—just to drink some nutrient-depleted, watered-down juice. If the packaging itself wasn't enough to make you juice for your kids, the simple fact is that while the juice sits on a store shelf, it will lose a good portion of its nutrients. Juicing and drinking right away will give your kids more nutrients than juice that has been on a shelf for three weeks or longer.

INSTILLING LIFELONG HEALTHY HABITS

One of the greatest lessons we can teach our kids is to make that connection between where their food originates and how it gets on our table. Real food comes from the earth. Kids who juice know where their juice is coming from. Making this connection will help kids to make healthy choices.

Kids who juice often and consistently, making a habit of it, will likely keep eating well the rest of their lives. Most kids develop their dietary preferences and habits by age ten. Guiding our kids to healthful eating and drinking by filling their plates and cups with healthy, nutritious foods daily will teach them to love eating that way.

Essential Juicing Ingredients

All you need to make a good juice is some fresh fruit. But here are some ideas to help you make the most of your juicer!

FRUITS

Fruits are high in water and therefore ideal to include with your juices. Juicing vegetables leaves a thick fluid, and adding some fruit helps to dilute it, making it more palatable and sweeter for kids.

- Apples
- Apricots
- Berries of all kinds
- Cherries
- Grapefruit
- Grapes
- Lemons and limes
- Oranges
- Peaches and nectarines
- Pears
- Plums

VEGETABLES

Adding vegetables to juices is not just a way to sneak them into your kids' diets. Vegetables can add a new flavor to juices, making even plain old apple juice interesting again. You can use any vegetables you can get your hands on. Even veggies that aren't quite ripe or ones that are past their prime are all suitable for juicing.

• Bell peppers	• Ginger	• String beans
• Broccoli	• Kale	• Sweet potatoes
• Cabbage	• Lettuce	• Swiss chard
• Carrots	• Potatoes	• Tomatoes
• Cauliflower	• Radishes	• Watercress
• Celery	• Spinach	• Wheat grass
• Cucumbers	• Squash	

WATER

While not necessary, water can dilute your juices to be just the right taste for your kids. When we started juicing, the new juice was a bit thicker than my kids were used to. We found that if we diluted the juice slightly with water and thinned it out a bit, our kids were more likely to drink it. Water also can help kids get that little extra hydration.

EXTRAS FOR FLAVOR

• Honey
• Vanilla extract

Health Benefits of Juices

Many people have medicine cabinets overflowing with antibiotics, pain relievers, stomach soothers, cough and cold medicines, and fever reducers. Unfortunately, this teaches children that they need to take a pill to treat common problems. What we should be teaching them is that our bodies are pretty good at fighting bugs, viruses, and inflammation with proper fuel. As they get the nutrients their cells are starving for, our kids will be equipped to fight and prevent many common illnesses.

THE BUILDING BLOCKS

Our bodies need vitamins and minerals to develop, grow, and do their job. The essential vitamins are only obtained through the food we eat, as our bodies cannot make these vitamins on their own. There are many kids today who are getting enough calories to stay alive but are not getting the proper vitamins they need to thrive. Raw fruits and vegetables are the answer to meeting all the nutrition needs we have. Cooking and preserving fruits and vegetables can destroy important nutrients. Juicing and eating them raw retains these vitamins that our kids need for growing.

Raw fruits and vegetables also retain important enzymes. Without the enzymes we get from plant foods, important system functioning is compromised. We need these enzymes to convert the food we eat into usable vitamins, proteins, and energy. Enzymes are vital in digestion, metabolism, and cell turnover. Cooking and preserving destroys these important enzymes, while eating fruits and vegetables fresh and juicing doesn't destroy them.

EATING A RAINBOW

The color in fruits and vegetables determine which phytochemicals and antioxidants are present. Each phytochemical has a different function. The darker and more colorful your foods are, the more packed they are with these phytochemicals. Green foods, such as spinach and kale, contain indole-3-carbinol, which has been shown to fight cancer. Red foods, such as strawberries, contain lycopene. Lycopene has been shown to lower cholesterol and reduce your risk for osteoporosis. Orange and yellow foods contain beta-carotene, which the body utilizes to make useable vitamin A. Purple and blue foods, like blueberries, contain anthocyanin. Anthocyanin can fight inflammation as well as bacterial infections. Even white foods have phytochemicals. White foods, like onions, contain quercetin. Quercetin is effective in boosting immunity. Because each plant color has a different function, eating a rainbow of fruits and vegetables has always been important in order to get all the health benefits possible. Eating a variety is easy with smoothies and juices as you can include a food with each color in every drink if you choose.

With the fiber removed, juice can be easy on the stomach for kids who struggle with digestion. Instead of breaking down fruits and vegetables to release and absorb the nutrients, juiced fruits and vegetables have nutrients that are easily absorbed.

Juicing is hydrating! Kids who are dehydrated can be confused, irritable, get headaches, get tired, or have very dry skin. No longer are the experts saying that everyone needs to drink eight to ten glasses of water per day. Water recommendations are now customized, as everyone is different. Juicing is a great way to get kids to drink and is filled with water from fruits and vegetables. Often they don't stop playing long enough to drink, but serving juices with meals and for snack time will help them hydrate. What's more, the water extracted from your fruits and veggies is filled with nutrients that tap water is missing.

Tips and Tricks to Making Juices Kids Will Eat

These strategies will help you encourage your kids to drink their homemade juices.

- **Start similar.** Kids who have been drinking commercial juices for any amount of time may be put off by the initial thickness and texture of homemade juices. Keep the texture similar to juice they are accustomed to drinking. Depending on your juicer, fruits and vegetables might juice differently, and different foods will yield a different amount of juice. Simply mixing a little ice-cold water into their juice will remind them of juices they are familiar with drinking.

- **Keep it cold!** Warm juices may not be appealing to kids or to you for that matter! Room temperature fruits and vegetables that are juiced are often too warm. Chilling the juice for a few minutes in the fridge or freezer makes juices more palatable.

- **Be creative—and let the kids play.** Let the kids create their own juices with any combination of fruits and vegetables they choose. My kids love to do this. They call it their experiments, and they make each other try what they've come up with. Our only rule is they must keep the ingredients edible! Recently, my ten-year-old took one peach and one apple to the juicer. She just wanted to see how it would turn out, and of course she loved it because she made it herself.

- **Make the drinks portable.** Drinking juice while running errands or bringing juice to school is easy with the cute take-along drinking cups available today. Thermos containers are getting new looks each school year. Fun characters now adorn once boring cups. Let each child have his or her own special cup that he or she can use when you go places, and include juices or smoothies that he or she enjoys.

- **Make serving fun.** Give your children the juice in new cups with crazy straws. Of all the tricks in this world, I thought this would be the least likely to work, but my kids loved it. I gave each of them their own new cups, with a straw attached to the bottom. They use it every time they make their juices.

- **Remember, kids want to be healthy.** In talking with kids and parents over the years, I found it interesting that most kids want to eat healthy food, although their parents continue to buy junk food. They often enjoy the taste of fruits and vegetables, and they want you to provide it for them. Smoothies and juices are the perfect vehicle for helping your kids get the fruits and vegetables they crave.

Purchasing a Juicer

Buying your first juicer may seem overwhelming because you want to get the best value. Juicers can vary greatly in price, but the most expensive juicers aren't always the best ones. In shopping for a juicer, consider customer feedback on sites like Amazon.com. Customers overall can be your best resources as their unedited reviews can give you vital information. For power, look for a juicer that has at least 0.5 horsepower. Check if the feed tube is large enough to fit at least a half an apple. You don't need to spend all morning chopping food to be juiced. Finally, assess how easy the juicer is to clean. With kids always on the go, cleaning your juicer should not be a big task.

2

Morning Sunshine:

DRINKS TO JUMP-START THE DAY

After a good night's sleep, most kids wake up famished. Their blood sugar is low, and their irritability may be high. Many families are busy in the morning, getting ready for school or work. Proper fueling up for the day doesn't need to be complicated or time-consuming, though. Smoothies and juices, infused with fruits, vegetables, antioxidants, nutrients, and even protein and carbohydrates, are a great way to help kids get their vitamin and mineral requirements for the day, even on the busiest of mornings.

Begin a new tradition in your family that eliminates traditional less-than-nutritious breakfasts, such as high-sugar cereals or pastries. Replace those breakfasts with something that will sustain your kids until lunch and help them focus through their morning classes or chores. A complete meal with eggs, whole-wheat toast, and a smoothie or juice can fuel their brains, energize their muscles, and provide the backbone for their continued growth and development. As kids get used to this new way of starting their day, they will look and feel great. The days of being sick, sluggish, and crashing at 10 A.M. will be a thing of the past.

Prep breakfast smoothies or juices the night before by washing, peeling, or cutting the foods you will be using. Keep these in the fridge for an even more streamlined and stress-free morning.

Gold Nugget Smoothie

The deep gold color of this smoothie is reminiscent of sunshine. The carrots in this sweet smoothie will support immunity, protect vision, and give kids the fiber they need each day.

FOUR 1-CUP SERVINGS

1 cup carrots
¾ cup pineapple juice
½ cup orange juice
1 tablespoon honey
½ cup plain or vanilla
   yogurt
1 cup ice cubes

1 Place carrots and pineapple juice in a high-powered blender, and blend until smooth. If carrots will not blend, soften them slightly in the microwave.

2 Add orange juice, honey, and yogurt, and blend until smooth.

3 Add ice cubes and blend one last time until smoothie is desired consistency.

CALORIES	FAT	PROTEIN	SODIUM	CARBOHYDRATES	SUGARS	FIBER
86	1 gram	2 grams	35 milligrams	18 grams	14 grams	1 gram

GREEN TIP: Washing Vegetables

Whether you purchase or grow your vegetables without pesticides, they still should be washed and cleaned thoroughly. Prepare yourself a vegetable wash by combining 1 cup each of water and vinegar, 1 tablespoon baking soda, and 2 tablespoons of lemon juice in a spray bottle. Tip spray bottle around and shake very gently to combine ingredients. Use the vegetable wash when bringing in carrots and other vegetables that may have soil residue. Rinse thoroughly with water and pat dry with a paper towel.

Over the Rainbow, Mango!

Put this smoothie together quickly in the morning by cutting up a fresh pineapple and portioning it into 1-cup containers in the fridge. Also, keep canned or frozen pineapple in the pantry for the off-season.

FOUR 1-CUP SERVINGS

½ cup dandelion greens
1 cup iceberg lettuce
1 ripe mango, peeled
  and pit removed
1 cup pineapple, cubed
1 orange, peeled
½ cup water

1 Combine the greens, lettuce, mango, pineapple, and orange in a blender.

2 Pour water over the fruits and vegetables.

3 Blend until all leafy greens are smooth and no longer visible. Keep adding enough water until the blender is able to make your smoothie smooth.

CALORIES	FAT	PROTEIN	SODIUM	CARBOHYDRATES	SUGARS	FIBER
71	0 grams	1 gram	3 milligrams	18 grams	15 grams	2 grams

GREEN TIP: No Waste

When using canned pineapple, never dump the pineapple juice down the drain. There are a myriad of ways to repurpose this sweet juice. Use leftover pineapple juice in this smoothie to replace part of the water. You can also pour pineapple juice into ice cube molds to add to water, other juices, or frosty smoothies. Pour leftover pineapple juice into ice pop molds for a summer treat, or use leftover pineapple juice for fruit salad to keep it fresh.

Inspector Nectar

Serve this peach smoothie with scrambled eggs and whole-wheat toast for a delicious breakfast. The protein, grains, veggies, and fruit make it a well-balanced meal.

FOUR 1-CUP SERVINGS

- 1 cup romaine lettuce
- 3 peaches, pitted, peel removed
- 1 banana, peeled
- ½ cup water

1 Combine lettuce, peaches, banana, and water in a blender, and blend.

2 Continue to add water until reaching desired consistency.

CALORIES	FAT	PROTEIN	SODIUM	CARBOHYDRATES	SUGARS	FIBER
71	0 grams	1 gram	1 milligram	18 grams	13 grams	3 grams

TIME SAVER TIP: Preparing Greens

Many of our greens go to waste. Spinach, kale, Swiss chard, and lettuce have a very short shelf life. However, your family is more likely to eat them before they go bad if they are washed and chopped and ready to eat. As soon as you return from the grocery store, wash, chop, and package your greens. Use one container for salads, one for cooking, and one for smoothies and juices. Bagging romaine lettuce in 1-cup baggies makes for easy and quick smoothies in the morning.

Citrus Sunshine Shake

Many kids like the tangy, sour tastes of citrus. The sour candy that is on the grocery store shelves proves it. The grapefruit and lemon in this smoothie is perfect for those kids who like to pucker up.

FOUR 1-CUP SERVINGS

1 cup baby spinach leaves
1 grapefruit, peeled
2 oranges, peeled
½" ginger, peeled
½ lemon, peeled
½–1 cup orange juice

1 Add spinach leaves, grapefruit, oranges, ginger, and lemon in a blender.

2 Add ½ cup orange juice to blender. Turn on high and blend until smooth.

3 If necessary, add the remaining juice until smoothie reaches the desired consistency.

CALORIES	FAT	PROTEIN	SODIUM	CARBOHYDRATES	SUGARS	FIBER
73	0 grams	2 grams	7 milligrams	18 grams	13 grams	3 grams

PICKY EATER: Make It Fun

Drinking this smoothie doesn't need to be routine or boring. Have certain smoothies that are fun for the kids to look forward to. For example, every time you make the Citrus Sunshine Shake, use a special cup that's reserved for special occasions. This could be a cup with a character that they like with a crazy straw. Changing it up and making it special will have picky kids looking forward to drinking their smoothies.

Lettuce Drink Bananas

This breakfast salad has such a variety of colors, you can be sure the nutrients will be diverse. This smoothie has green, red, blue, yellow, and white foods that incorporate antioxidants of every kind.

FOUR 1-CUP SERVINGS

1 cup iceberg lettuce
1 pint strawberries
1 pint blueberries
1 banana, peeled
½ cup vanilla almond milk
½ cup ice cubes

1 Put all ingredients except ice in a blender, and blend until smooth.

2 Add ice and blend again until desired consistency.

CALORIES	FAT	PROTEIN	SODIUM	CARBOHYDRATES	SUGARS	FIBER
136	2 grams	3 grams	24 milligrams	28 grams	16 grams	5 grams

NUTRITION NEWS: Iceberg Lettuce

If you've heard iceberg lettuce was a nutrient weakling, you may have been misled. Iceberg lettuce does have a lot of water and very few calories. This, however, is what is so amazing about it. 100 calories of iceberg lettuce has almost 9 grams of fiber, 6 grams of protein, and ½ gram of healthy fats. The trouble is trying to eat 100 calories of iceberg lettuce!

Raspberry Rascals

Worried about protein? Picky eaters won't have a problem with this smoothie. The high protein amount in Greek-style yogurts makes this smoothie a perfect drink to start your kids' day.

FOUR 1-CUP SERVINGS

1 cup iceberg lettuce
2 pints raspberries
1 banana, peeled
½ cup rice milk
½ cup Greek-style
  yogurt

1 Place lettuce, raspberries, banana, and rice milk in a blender. Blend until smooth.

2 Add Greek-style yogurt and blend.

CALORIES	FAT	PROTEIN	SODIUM	CARBOHYDRATES	SUGARS	FIBER
125	1 gram	6 grams	30 milligrams	25 grams	12 grams	9 grams

DIY: Rice Milk

Making your own rice milk is as simple as making smoothies. Combine 2 cups water, ¼ cup brown rice, a dash of vanilla extract, and a dash of honey. Blend until the consistency is like milk. Store the rice milk in a glass jar in the fridge, for up to 1 week. Shake well when ready to drink or use.

Brainy Banana

Wake up to almond milk! This smoothie uses almond milk, a great alternative for those who are lactose intolerant or have other milk allergies. Or for those mornings you are just fresh out of milk (see the sidebar "DIY: Almond Milk" in this recipe to learn how to make your own).

FOUR 1-CUP SERVINGS

1 cup romaine lettuce
2 bananas, peeled
1 pint strawberries
1 pint blueberries
2 cups almond milk

1 Add all ingredients except almond milk to a blender. Blend.

2 Slowly add the almond milk and blend until smooth enough to drink.

CALORIES	FAT	PROTEIN	SODIUM	CARBOHYDRATES	SUGARS	FIBER
145	1 gram	3 grams	9 milligrams	33 grams	18 grams	6 grams

DIY: Almond Milk

Making your own almond milk ensures you'll serve a creamier and tastier version than you'll find in stores—and you can be sure there are no preservatives or additives. Use blanched raw almonds, or soak regular almonds until the skins fall off. Once they are skinless, immerse in water overnight, or at least 4 hours. Strain the water, and blend the soft almonds with 1½ cups of water in a blender. Add 2½ more cups of water and blend again till smooth. You may also add vanilla and a sweetener if you choose. For thinner milk, strain through a cheesecloth.

Bye-Bye Blackberry Pie

This blackberry smoothie is delicious with a plate of French toast for breakfast. Drink with your breakfast, or serve your French toast with the smoothie instead of syrup. Add any leftover whole blackberries to top it off.

FOUR 1-CUP SERVINGS

1 cup spinach
2 pints blackberries
1 banana, peeled
½ lemon, peeled
1 cup Greek-style plain
   yogurt

1 Place all ingredients in blender.

2 Blend until consistency is smooth and desired texture is achieved.

CALORIES	FAT	PROTEIN	SODIUM	CARBOHYDRATES	SUGARS	FIBER
125	1 gram	9 grams	31 milligrams	24 grams	13 grams	9 grams

PICKY EATER:
Match Familiar Flavors with New Flavors

As you introduce your children to new flavors and foods, combine them with old familiar ones. This smoothie is great for kids who love sweet bananas and blackberries but haven't given lemons a chance yet. The subtle flavor of the sour lemon will give them a taste of the lemon without scaring them away. The more often they try new flavors, textures, and tastes, the more likely they will be to accept new foods.

A Day at the Peach

With a serving and a half of fruits and vegetables in each cup, this smoothie has kids on track to consume the recommended five servings a day.

FOUR 1-CUP SERVINGS

1 cup watercress
3 peaches, pitted
1 cup strawberries
1 orange, peeled
¼" ginger, peeled
2 cups water

1 Place watercress, peaches, strawberries, orange, ginger, and 1 cup water in a blender, and blend until well combined.

2 Add remaining 1 cup water, and blend until reaching desired consistency.

CALORIES	FAT	PROTEIN	SODIUM	CARBOHYDRATES	SUGARS	FIBER
72	0 grams	2 grams	4 milligrams	18 grams	14 grams	3 grams

DIY: Canning Peaches

Peach season is too short. The peach trees are ripe and the fruit is perfect for only a few weeks. Then it's peach famine until the following year. You can stretch the season all year by canning your own peaches. Canning yourself, rather than purchasing canned peaches from the store, is healthier for you and your kids. You'll know exactly what's in your peaches, how long they've been on a shelf, and the materials they are being stored in. While canning peaches can be a lengthy process, it's a great tradition to start with your family as you'll enjoy the fruits of your labor all year long.

Dazzling Date Drinkers

This breakfast smoothie will take the place of any sweetened cereal or heavy syrup. The dates, banana, and papaya lend a natural sweetness that can't be compared.

FOUR 1-CUP SERVINGS

1 cup watercress
2 cups papaya
1 banana, peeled
1 date, pitted
Pulp of 1 vanilla bean
1 tablespoon raw hemp seed protein
2 cups almond milk

1 Combine watercress, papaya, banana, date, vanilla bean, hemp protein, and 1 cup almond milk in a blender. Blend until well combined.

2 Add remaining 1 cup almond milk, and continue to blend until smooth and light.

CALORIES	FAT	PROTEIN	SODIUM	CARBOHYDRATES	SUGARS	FIBER
142	2 grams	5 grams	68 milligrams	27 grams	18 grams	3 grams

NUTRITION NEWS: Hemp Protein—What Is It?

Hemp seeds are a valuable food for kids who may be picky eaters. Unlike many plant-based proteins, hemp seeds have all the essential amino acids. This is great news for parents having a hard time getting their kids to eat much food. Hemp seeds are also high in the good fats, like omega-3s. They're high in fiber, and contain vitamin E and other minerals. Hemp seeds are generally found in health food stores next to specialty flours such as flax meal or soy flours.

Big Banana Dipper

Try this high-fiber, high-flavor smoothie with a plate full of scrambled eggs and a slice of whole-wheat toast. All your food groups will be covered with fruit, veggies, dairy, protein, and whole grains.

FOUR 1-CUP SERVINGS

2 cups romaine lettuce

4 apricots, pits removed

2 apples, peeled and cored

1 banana, peeled

2 cups plain yogurt

½ cup orange juice

1 Place romaine lettuce, apricots, apples, bananas, 1 cup yogurt, and orange juice in a blender, and blend for 30 seconds.

2 Add remaining 1 cup yogurt, and blend again until smooth, about 60–90 seconds.

CALORIES	FAT	PROTEIN	SODIUM	CARBOHYDRATES	SUGARS	FIBER
175	4 grams	6 gram	59 milligrams	31 grams	24 grams	3 grams

NUTRITION NEWS: Fiber

Fiber is an important nutrient for kids. Fiber has no calories, it prevents constipation, and it lowers the risk for heart disease and diabetes. Kids should consume 5 grams of fiber plus their age in grams. This would mean a six-year-old should have 11 grams of fiber (5 grams + 6 [age] grams). This smoothie is a great start as each serving contains 3 grams of fiber.

Carotene Quencher

One look at this orange smoothie and you will know it's bursting with beta-carotene. Watching them drinking their beta-carotene up for breakfast is reassuring, in case your kids don't eat the carrots that went into their lunchbox.

FOUR 1-CUP SERVINGS

2 cups cantaloupe, rind and seeds removed
2 bananas, peeled
1 cup almond milk
1 cup ice

1 Place cantaloupe, bananas, and ½ cup almond milk in a blender, and blend for 30 seconds.

2 Add remaining almond milk and ice, and continue to blend until smoothie is well mixed and frosty.

CALORIES	FAT	PROTEIN	SODIUM	CARBOHYDRATES	SUGARS	FIBER
111	1 gram	3 grams	44 milligrams	24 grams	16 grams	3 grams

PICKY EATER: Kids Eat What Tastes Good

Children who refuse to eat food generally don't care for the way it tastes, at least for that day. However, kids who give something a try and find the flavor is enjoyable will continue to eat that thing. The take-away message here is to learn how to prepare foods that taste good. Rather than raw broccoli, roast some with Parmesan cheese. Rather than plain pancakes, add berries to them. Mostly, rather than a plain glass of almond milk, add cantaloupe and banana as in this smoothie, and enhance the flavor for picky kids to enjoy.

The Yummy Honey Bunny

Your children will be surprised there are any vegetables in this smoothie at all. If it weren't for the green color giving it away, the sweetness would be enough to convince them they were eating dessert.

FOUR 1-CUP SERVINGS

2 cups honeydew melon, rind and seeds removed

1 cup spinach

2 bananas, peeled

½ cup plain yogurt

1 cup of ice

1 Combine honeydew melon, spinach, bananas, and yogurt in a blender. Blend on high for about 20-30 seconds.

2 Add ice and blend until all ingredients are well combined.

CALORIES	FAT	PROTEIN	SODIUM	CARBOHYDRATES	SUGARS	FIBER
104	1 gram	2 grams	36 milligrams	23 grams	16 grams	2 grams

DIY: Teaching Kids to Use a Knife

Helping your kids learn prep skills such as cutting is a big step in independence for them, and it encourages them to prepare and appreciate healthy food. This recipe uses soft fruits such as honeydew melon and bananas, which are perfect for little hands to learn with. With your child positioned high enough to be over the food and have a good view of what he is doing, place a peeled banana on a cutting board, show him the proper use of the knife, and assist as he cuts the banana into 1" chunks. Let him put the banana in the blender for you. He will be on his way to cutting bigger and tougher vegetables and fruits in no time.

Sweet Pear Maiden

This cold, creamy pear smoothie is delicious with some hot cinnamon oatmeal in the morning. Chop some of the pear to use in the smoothie, and use the rest to top the cinnamon oatmeal.

FOUR 1-CUP SERVINGS

1 cup spinach

4 pears, peeled and cored

2 bananas, peeled

2 cups vanilla yogurt

1 cup ice

1 Place spinach, pears, banana, and yogurt in a blender, and blend until smooth.

2 Add the ice, and blend until the desired texture is achieved.

CALORIES	FAT	PROTEIN	SODIUM	CARBOHYDRATES	SUGARS	FIBER
193	2 grams	7 grams	87 milligrams	39 grams	30 grams	5 grams

PICKY EATER: Choosing Pears

With over 3,000 varieties of pear growing around the world, knowing which ones to get may make the difference between a child loving and hating pears. The Red Anjou pear is described as aromatic and juicy. The Bartlett pear is super juicy. The Bosc pear tastes like honey, while the Comice pear tastes like butter. Don't dismiss a child's dislike for pears until she has had a chance to taste different kinds. She may like one variety and not another. Don't give up!

Kickin' Cantaloupe

Fresh cantaloupe juice dripping on your children's clean school clothes will no longer be a problem when you make it into a smoothie to drink from a straw. Keep your mornings clean by serving up smoothies instead of whole fruit.

FOUR 1-CUP SERVINGS

1 cup romaine lettuce

2 cups pineapple

2 cups cantaloupe, rind removed

1 cup water

1 cup ice

1 Place romaine, pineapple, cantaloupe, and 1 cup water in a blender, and blend until smooth.

2 Add the ice, and continue to blend until smooth and desired consistency is reached.

CALORIES	FAT	PROTEIN	SODIUM	CARBOHYDRATES	SUGARS	FIBER
70	0 grams	1 gram	14 milligrams	18 grams	14 grams	2 grams

DIY: Cantaloupe

When choosing a cantaloupe at the supermarket or farmers' market, look for a fruit that has a sweet melon smell to it and is soft to a small amount of pressure. If a cantaloupe isn't fully ripe, it can ripen sitting on your kitchen counter at room temperature for up to four days. After cutting into a cantaloupe, it should be stored in a refrigerator. Or scoop out the flesh with a melon baller and freeze until you are ready to prepare your smoothie. Dispose of the rinds in a compost pile.

Prancing Pineapples

Heading back to school after a summer in the fresh outdoors requires some extra vitamin C to fight those bugs kids share in a cramped classroom. This vitamin C–packed smoothie is the perfect drink before sending your kids back to school.

FOUR 1-CUP SERVINGS

1 cup radicchio leaves
2 tangerines, peeled
2 cups pineapple
1 cup grapefruit
1 cup orange juice
1 cup ice

1 Place all ingredients except ice in a blender. Blend until smooth.

2 Add ice, then turn blender on again until drink is smooth and well incorporated.

CALORIES	FAT	PROTEIN	SODIUM	CARBOHYDRATES	SUGARS	FIBER
121	0 grams	2 grams	5 milligrams	30 grams	23 grams	3 grams

DIY: Cutting a Pineapple

Cutting a pineapple can be intimidating, especially for those of us who have been buying pineapple in a can for so long. When you do purchase a fresh pineapple, follow these simple instructions. First, lay the pineapple on its side on a cutting board. With a sharp knife, cut off both ends of the pineapple, the stalk end as well as the bottom. Stand the pineapple up on its cut bottom, and slice your knife down each edge to remove the outer skin. Lay the pineapple on its side again, and slice discs out of the pineapple. With each round of pineapple, cut the tough center out to make it more enjoyable.

Outrageous Orange Explosion

Enjoy the burst of orange in this smoothie with some cold Swiss muesli. Add some nuts and dried fruit to the muesli, and breakfast will be unforgettable. Good fats, complex carbs, and proteins round out this balanced meal.

FOUR 1-CUP SERVINGS

1 cup iceberg lettuce
3 oranges, peeled
½ cup coconut milk

1 Combine all ingredients in a blender, and blend until smoothie is desired consistency.

2 Serve.

CALORIES	FAT	PROTEIN	SODIUM	CARBOHYDRATES	SUGARS	FIBER
62	2 grams	1 gram	5 milligrams	12 grams	9 grams	3 grams

NUTRITION NEWS: Super Oranges

Oranges have a well-deserved reputation for being high in vitamin C. One orange provides 116 percent of the recommended daily value. However, oranges have more health benefits than just the immunity protection the vitamin C offers. The phytonutrients present in an orange allow the vitamin C to be used more effectively in your body than if you were to take it as an isolated supplement. These same phytonutrients also have been shown to have anti-inflammatory benefits and may contribute to lower blood pressure as well as lower cholesterol. The whole orange, as blended up in this smoothie, has been shown to be more protective than the juice alone.

Nutty and Nice

The banana lovers in your house will ask for this smoothie for special weekend mornings. Be ready by always having bananas on hand, and you won't disappoint the kids.

FOUR 1-CUP SERVINGS

½ cup Greek-style yogurt
1 cup iceberg lettuce
2 banana, peeled
1 cup vanilla-flavored almond milk

1 Combine yogurt, lettuce, and banana in a blender, and blend until smooth.

2 Add almond milk, and blend until smoothie is desired consistency.

CALORIES	FAT	PROTEIN	SODIUM	CARBOHYDRATES	SUGARS	FIBER
103	1 gram	6 grams	45 milligrams	19 grams	11 grams	2 grams

TIME SAVER TIP: Make Ahead!

Making smoothies for breakfast isn't very time-consuming, but it does require a small amount of prepping of the fruits and vegetables. Eliminate this extra time altogether on busy days, and prepare this smoothie the night before. Keep the smoothie in the fridge in a cup that contains a lid and a coiled wire whisk inside, often called a blender bottle. This will allow you to grab the premade smoothie, give it a shake, and then head out the door.

The Green Gatsby

When kids start their day with this high-fiber smoothie, digestion isn't the only thing that improves. The fiber in this smoothie will also keep kids full until lunch, which helps them concentrate in school.

FOUR 1-CUP SERVINGS

1 cup spinach

2 green apples, peeled
   and cored

1 banana, peeled

1 cup water

1 Combine spinach, apples, banana, and ½ cup water in a blender, and blend until smooth.

2 Add remaining ½ cup water, and continue to blend until desired consistency is achieved.

CALORIES	FAT	PROTEIN	SODIUM	CARBOHYDRATES	SUGARS	FIBER
67	0 grams	1 gram	6 milligrams	17 grams	12 grams	2 grams

MAKE IT FUN: Smoothies for Holidays

Colorful drinks are as fun for kids as the holiday itself. This smoothie could both be part of the décor for St. Patty's Day as well as the treat. Pink smoothies, with beets, are perfect for Valentine's Day. Orange smoothies, made with cantaloupe, would complement Halloween nicely. Red or blue smoothies made with raspberries or blueberries are terrific for the Fourth of July.

Purrr-fect Pears

This breakfast smoothie is a fruit salad in a glass, without the chopping and cutting. Including fruit for breakfast has never been easier than throwing everything in a blender.

FOUR 1-CUP SERVINGS

1 cup romaine lettuce

2 pears, peeled and cored

1 apple, peeled and cored

1 banana, peeled

½ cup water

1 Combine all ingredients in a blender. Blend on high until smooth.

2 Continue to blend, while pushing food onto blades with damper if necessary, until smoothie is consistency desired.

CALORIES	FAT	PROTEIN	SODIUM	CARBOHYDRATES	SUGARS	FIBER
65	0 grams	1 gram	1 milligram	17 grams	11 grams	3 grams

DIY: Starting a Compost Pile

With all the added fruits and vegetables you'll be eating in your house, there will be more scraps and waste. Banana peels and apple cores can all be thrown into a compost pile to be recycled and used for growing more food. Kids will enjoy starting a compost pile. Simply purchase a compost container from a local hardware store. Containers made for composting have holes in them for drainage and circulation. Add grass clippings, fruit and vegetable scraps, leaves, hay, and cardboard or newspaper. Rotate and mix the container to keep it aerated, and don't forget to keep it moist. Your compost will be ready in 3–4 weeks to be used to plant veggies and fertilize soil.

Lime Lovin' Lions

Cereals these days have as many as 8-16 grams of sugar per serving. Unfortunately, all of the sugar is the refined, processed type. Replace breakfast cereals with this smoothie and give your kids natural sugar from fruit rather than processed sugar from cereal.

FOUR 1-CUP SERVINGS

1 cup spinach
2 limes, peeled and
   deseeded
1 banana, peeled
½ cup orange juice

1 Place spinach, limes, and banana in a blender, and blend as well as possible.

2 Add the juice, and blend until all food is processed and smooth.

CALORIES	FAT	PROTEIN	SODIUM	CARBOHYDRATES	SUGARS	FIBER
53	0 grams	1 gram	8 milligrams	14 grams	7 grams	2 grams

PICKY EATER: Relax!

Breakfast is not traditionally a meal that we sit down and enjoy. We are either stressed out and running around, or our kids are distracted by morning cartoons. Wake up twenty minutes early and sit down to relax at breakfast with your family. Enjoy the company of each other, turn off the distractions, and drink your smoothies together. Kids who are less stressed out and distracted are more likely to consume their breakfast with less nagging from the parents.

Bloomin' Blueberry

Jump-start your kids' engines with this high-energy shake instead of a morning breakfast bar. The nutrients in the banana and blueberries will wake a child up with a more stable mood than a high-sugar meal.

FOUR 1-CUP SERVINGS

1 cup iceberg lettuce
2 pints blueberries
1 banana, peeled
½ cup rice milk

1 Place iceberg, blueberries, banana, and ¼ cup rice milk in a blender, and blend on high until smooth.

2 Add the remaining ¼ cup rice milk, and blend until the smoothie is the desired consistency.

CALORIES	FAT	PROTEIN	SODIUM	CARBOHYDRATES	SUGARS	FIBER
181	2 grams	4 grams	31 milligrams	36 grams	20 grams	7 grams

DIY: Pick Your Own Blueberries

Many farms across the country allow for individuals and families to come pick their own fruit and vegetables. A popular "pick your own" field is a blueberry patch. Not only does this save money because you are doing all the work, but it also is fun for the kids. At some farms, you can even snack on the berries while you pick! Use the blueberries for this smoothie or for muffins, pancakes, juicing, or fruit salads. Head over to *www.pickyourown.org* for a complete list of places in your state that offer this.

Wise Old Peach

Many nutrients are found in apple skins and just below the skin. For this smoothie, leave the apple skin intact to get all the benefits the apple provides.

FOUR 1-CUP SERVINGS

1 cup radicchio leaves
3 peaches, pitted
2 apples, cored
2 cups almond milk

1 Combine radicchio leaves, peaches, apples, and 1 cup almond milk in a blender, and blend for 30 seconds.

2 Remove the lid and push food down onto the blender blades, then add remaining almond milk.

3 Blend until smoothie is desired consistency.

CALORIES	FAT	PROTEIN	SODIUM	CARBOHYDRATES	SUGARS	FIBER
150	3 grams	5 grams	64 milligrams	29 grams	22 grams	4 grams

GREEN TIP: Organic Labeling

Just because produce isn't labeled "organic" doesn't always mean it's not. Talk to the farmers and ask about their farming practices. Some farmers comply with organic standards but cannot afford to be certified. For appropriately labeled foods, labels for 100 percent organic foods must contain only organic ingredients and processes. Those labeled "organic" must be 95 percent processed with organic methods. Organic produce is grown without the use of pesticides, synthetic fertilizers, genetically modified organisms, or ionizing radiation.

Jack and Ginger

It's never fun to wake up a little queasy before school. Whether your child is nervous or just uneasy, this ginger smoothie will tame that troubled tummy.

FOUR 1-CUP SERVINGS

1 cup romaine lettuce

3 apples, cored and
    peeled

1 tablespoon ginger,
    peeled

2 cups soy milk

1 Take romaine lettuce, apples, ginger, and 1 cup soy milk, and place in blender. Blend until smooth.

2 Add remaining soy milk, and blend until smoothie is the texture your kids enjoy.

CALORIES	FAT	PROTEIN	SODIUM	CARBOHYDRATES	SUGARS	FIBER
130	2 grams	5 grams	63 milligrams	24 grams	17 grams	3 grams

DIY: Drying Ginger

There are two ways of storing fresh ginger. One is to freeze or refrigerate the entire root in a plastic bag. Grate or chop away ginger as needed. The second way, for a longer shelf life, is to dry the ginger yourself. The flavor of fresh-dried ginger beats the dried ground ginger on the spice shelf every time. Take a fresh gingerroot and wash and dry it. Peel the skin away gently with a vegetable peeler. With a grater, grate the ginger onto a wire or mesh screen. Place the screen in a dehydrator for 2–3 days. You can also dry ginger in an oven over low heat if you do not own a dehydrator. Set your oven to its lowest setting, prefer-ably 130°F. Place the ginger on wire racks for 10–15 hours, rotating the ginger every 3–4 hours. Store dried ginger in a plastic bag until ready to use.

Lightning McLemon

The flavor of this lemony berry drink is a great vehicle for getting some digestion-friendly flax meal into kids. The fiber from all the fruits, vegetables, and flax will help their digestive systems work properly.

FOUR 1-CUP SERVINGS

2 cups blueberries
1 cup spinach
2 bananas, peeled
½ lemon, peeled
1 tablespoon flax meal
2 cups orange juice

1 Combine blueberries, spinach, bananas, lemon, flax meal, and 1 cup orange juice in a blender, and blend on low for 30 seconds.

2 Add remaining orange juice, and continue to blend until smoothie is desired consistency.

CALORIES	FAT	PROTEIN	SODIUM	CARBOHYDRATES	SUGARS	FIBER
194	2 grams	4 grams	16 milligrams	43 grams	25 grams	6 grams

PICKY EATER: Stick to a Schedule

Sticking to a regular feeding schedule is important if you are trying to avoid a picky eater struggle. When mealtime comes, kids should be hungry. When children are hungry, they will eat or try almost anything you offer. Kids who are permitted to snack all day almost never have a chance to be hungry and therefore are justified in their aversion to tasting and trying new foods. Create a schedule for your kids. Depending on their ages, you may start your day with a smoothie and toast, have lunch around noon, and offer a midafternoon snack with some protein, like nuts or a hard-boiled egg, when they come home from school. Then, have no food available until dinnertime.

Bursting Broccoli Breakfast

*Broccoli's ability to clean out contaminates has caused some to label it
a detox food. The great part about this smoothie is the broccoli works
with our bodies' natural abilities to detox, eliminate, and neutralize.*

FOUR 1-CUP SERVINGS

2 large kale leaves
1 cup broccoli
2 apples, peeled and
    cored
1 carrot, peeled
½ lemon, peeled
1 tablespoon flax meal
2 cups pomegranate juice

1 Place kale, broccoli, apples, carrot, lemon,
flax meal, and 1 cup juice in a high-powered
blender. Blend on low for 30 seconds.

2 Add remaining 1 cup juice, and blend until
smoothie is desired consistency.

CALORIES	FAT	PROTEIN	SODIUM	CARBOHYDRATES	SUGARS	FIBER
138	1 gram	2 grams	37 milligrams	32 grams	25 grams	3 grams

GREEN TIP: Hitting the Farmers' Market

Most of the produce in this smoothie can be purchased at your local farmers'
market. A farmers' market has several advantages over purchasing produce at
the grocery store. The produce is usually picked ripe, close to the time of sale,
as opposed to fruits and vegetables being picked several weeks before they are
ripe and allowed to ripen across the country in transport. Produce purchased
straight from the farmer eliminates costs incurred by transporting and storing
food. Ask the farmers about their growing practices. It could be that they don't
use pesticides and could be considered organic but simply haven't paid the
high price to be certified. Most of all, heading to the farmers' market with your
kids gives them a chance to see firsthand where whole foods come from and
learn from the farmers themselves.

Breakfast Banana Band

This breakfast smoothie has a bit of everything. It has a little vitamin C to start the day, a little potassium to keep kids going, a little lycopene for protection from heart disease, some fiber for regulation, and a big taste, for enjoyment.

FOUR 1-CUP SERVINGS

1 cup romaine lettuce

1 cup pineapple, peeled, and cored

1 pint strawberries

1 banana, peeled

1 cup Greek-style yogurt

1 Place romaine, pineapple, strawberries, banana, and ½ cup yogurt in a blender, and blend for 30 seconds.

2 Add remaining ½ cup yogurt, and blend until smoothie is desired consistency.

CALORIES	FAT	PROTEIN	SODIUM	CARBOHYDRATES	SUGARS	FIBER
105	0 grams	7 grams	26 milligrams	20 grams	14 grams	3 grams

NUTRITION NEWS: Greek-Style Yogurt

Greek-style yogurt has become very popular over the last few years, with good reason. For starters, Greek-style yogurt generally has double the amount of protein as regular yogurt. This is good news for vegetarians and parents who are concerned their kids aren't eating enough protein. Greek-style yogurt also has at least five active cultures, including acidophilus, which supports and improves gut health and reduces diarrhea. Greek-style yogurt, with its live cultures and high protein, also has less sugar and more calcium. It has all the good things we like about yogurt, magnified.

Spanky's Spinach Smoothie

Start your kids' day off with a true green smoothie. This one offers the benefits of protein, the nutrients of fruits, the minerals in vegetables, and the taste of a milkshake.

FOUR ½-CUP SERVINGS

3 cups packed baby spinach
2 cups frozen peaches
1 cup frozen mangoes
½ cup skim milk
1 cup orange juice
1 cup vanilla yogurt
1 block silken tofu

1 Take spinach, peaches, mangoes, skim milk, orange juice, and vanilla yogurt, and place in blender. Blend on high for about 20–30 seconds.

2 Add the tofu, and blend again until smooth.

CALORIES	FAT	PROTEIN	SODIUM	CARBOHYDRATES	SUGARS	FIBER
174	2 grams	8 grams	84 milligrams	33 grams	28 grams	3 grams

DIY: Making Your Own Yogurt

Making your yogurt is much less expensive than purchasing commercial yogurt sold at the store. When you make your own from scratch, you can also decide how to flavor it, without adding sugar. You can also control the quality of your milk. If you prefer yogurt without antibiotics or hormones, making your yogurt from that type of milk is possible. Warm ½ gallon milk to 185°F. Cool the milk down to 110°F and stir in 2–3 tablespoons plain yogurt. Cover with a warm towel and let sit for 7–10 hours. Strain if too watery.

Zesty Lemon

Even when you're serving your drinks on the go, they can still be special.
Add some lemon and lime zest to this drink, and top it off with a cherry.
This is one refreshing drink that will be appreciated by your kids.

FOUR 1-CUP SERVINGS

1 grapefruit, peeled
½ pineapple, peeled
  and cored
1 orange, peeled
½ lemon, peeled
½ lime, peeled
2 cups orange juice

1 Take grapefruit, pineapple, orange, lemon, lime, and 1 cup orange juice, and place in a blender. Blend until smooth.

2 Add remaining 1 cup orange juice, and blend until smoothie is desired consistency.

CALORIES	FAT	PROTEIN	SODIUM	CARBOHYDRATES	SUGARS	FIBER
158	0 grams	2 grams	4 milligrams	40 grams	29 grams	4 grams

MAKE IT FUN: Eat As a Family

Whether it's breakfast or dinner, families should be eating together. Studies show families who eat together have kids who are less likely to take drugs or use alcohol. Kids in families who eat together create stronger family bonds, the kids do better in school, kids learn important manners and skills, teens are less likely to be promiscuous, families save money, and the kids are happier. With all the research out about eating together, there is no question it should be something each family strives for. Busy families can't always get together for dinner, but sometimes breakfast is an option. Make your smoothies together, and sit down while you drink them together and interact with each other.

Big Apple Lemon Circus

A tangy touch of lemon and a pinch of sweet apple and banana is all you need to hide the spinach in this smoothie. Your kids will be thanking you for having breakfast ready, and you'll be thanking them for drinking it.

FOUR 1-CUP SERVINGS

1 cup spinach
3 apples, peeled and
  cored
1 banana, peeled
½ lemon, peeled
2 cups apple juice

1 Take spinach, apples, banana, lemon, and 1 cup apple juice, and place in a blender. Blend on high for 30 seconds.

2 Add remaining apple juice, and blend until smoothie is desired consistency.

CALORIES	FAT	PROTEIN	SODIUM	CARBOHYDRATES	SUGARS	FIBER
145	0 grams	1 gram	11 milligrams	37 grams	28 grams	3 grams

PICKY EATER: Getting Kids Hydrated

It's the middle of summer, and kids are playing their little hearts out. They don't want to stop playing just for a lousy drink of water. They really believe they are going to miss something important if they take a break. So make it easy for them to hydrate at will. Fill smoothies and juice cups for your kids as well as the neighbors, and bring them out. Give them personalized water bottles that they are willing to carry around and use. Kids love using and having their own hydration packs, even if they aren't hiking. Have water easy to access. Whether it's on the front of your fridge or you have a step stool at the sink, make it possible for them to get drinks on their own.

Sippin' Extreme Cider

It doesn't have to be winter to drink apple cider. This cold apple cider is delicious with a breakfast bar or homemade granola bar.

FOUR 1-CUP SERVINGS

2 pears, cored and peeled
2 apples, cored
½" gingerroot
½ teaspoon cinnamon
2 cups water

1 Place pears, apples, ginger, cinnamon, and 1 cup water in a blender, and blend until smooth.

2 Add remaining 1 cup water, and blend until desired consistency.

CALORIES	FAT	PROTEIN	SODIUM	CARBOHYDRATES	SUGARS	FIBER
60	0 grams	1 gram	0 milligrams	16 grams	11 grams	3 grams

DIY: Cleaning Your Blender

Cleaning your blender should be done after each use. However, certain care should be taken to give your blender the longest life possible. Cleaning the pitcher right after use is the best way to avoid scrubbing dried food out. Immediately following use, fill it with warm water and a squirt of dish soap. Place the blender back on the base and pulse for a few seconds. The soapy water will clean the blades and the sides of the pitcher. Rinse thoroughly with warm water and air dry. Then, unplug your blender and wipe the base with a damp cloth. For hard-to-reach places, wipe with a cotton swab around a toothpick or use a Q-tip.

Baby's Berry Blizzard

Big kids don't need to be the only ones enjoying a healthful smoothie. Older babies (one-year-olds and up) can also enjoy a creamy treat. Keep it thick, and serve with a spoon, and your baby will be grabbing the spoon straight from your hand.

FOUR 1-CUP SERVINGS

1 cup spinach
2 bananas, peeled
1 cup blueberries
1 cup strawberries
1 cup plain yogurt

1 Combine spinach, bananas, blueberries, straw-berries, and yogurt into a blender, and blend until smooth.

2 Continue to blend until desired consistency.

CALORIES	FAT	PROTEIN	SODIUM	CARBOHYDRATES	SUGARS	FIBER
137	3 grams	4 grams	38 milligrams	26 grams	15 grams	4 grams

NUTRITION NEWS: Yogurt

Adding yogurt to this smoothie does more than make it creamy and delicious. Yogurt is good for kids as well! Yogurt is a good source of calcium, a mineral kids need for growing strong bones. Yogurt also is a good source of other nutri-ents, such as phosphorus, vitamin B, protein, potassium, and zinc. While many other foods also contain these nutrients, yogurt is special because it contains live bacteria that is helpful to a good digestive system. These live bacteria have also been shown in studies to strengthen immunity and help you live longer.

Microbursts Melon

Let your children drink this smoothie on the first day of school. The calming fruits combined with the ginger will put anxious kids at ease and help their stress to melt away.

FOUR 1-CUP SERVINGS

1 cup arugula
½ cantaloupe, rind and seeds removed
½ honeydew melon, rind and seeds removed
1 tangerine, peeled
½" ginger, peeled
1 cup orange juice
1 tablespoon flax meal

1 Place arugula, cantaloupe, honeydew melon, tangerine, ginger, and ½ cup orange juice in a blender, and blend until well combined.

2 Add remaining orange juice and flax meal. Blend until smoothie is desired consistency.

CALORIES	FAT	PROTEIN	SODIUM	CARBOHYDRATES	SUGARS	FIBER
126	1 gram	3 grams	37 milligrams	29 grams	24 grams	3 grams

NUTRITION NEWS: Leafy Greens

Greens that are great in salads include arugula, romaine, baby spinach, iceberg lettuce, and red-leaf lettuce. These greens are mild in flavor, and generally not classified as bitter, the way other vegetables taste to children. All these greens can be used to make delicious salads, but they can also be used in smoothies. The benefits to adding greens to smoothies are that they are low in calories yet bursting with nutrients. Among many unidentified antioxidants and phytochemicals, salad greens also contain vitamin A, vitamin C, calcium, and potassium.

Peachy Keen Morning Machine

Nothing starts kids' engines better in the morning than a glass full of manganese. This trace mineral, contained in high doses in pineapple, is an essential coenzyme for energy production.

FOUR ½-CUP SERVINGS

1½ cups fresh pine-
apple
1 peach, pitted
3 tablespoons water

1 Place both the pineapple and the peach in a juicer, and run through the juicer.

2 Mix thoroughly together. If juice is too thick, dilute with the water a tablespoon at a time until it's the consistency your kids like.

CALORIES	FAT	PROTEIN	SODIUM	CARBOHYDRATES	SUGARS	FIBER
45	0 grams	1 gram	1 milligram	12 grams	9 grams	1 gram

TIME SAVER TIP: Stress-Free Mornings

Feeding kids and getting them out the door in the morning can be challenging. For less mess and stress, prepare juices the night before and store in the fridge. No spills to wipe or appliances to clean when you are trying to get out the door. This is the perfect recipe for storing overnight. The citrus in the pineapple keeps the drink from browning better than an apple-based juice. Fresh, home-made juices can be stored safely in the fridge for 24–48 hours.

Morning Melon Magic

After an overnight fast, this fresh juice is the perfect way to get kids going in the morning. The refreshing zing of cucumber mixed with the sweet taste from the melons will wake them up and jump-start their engines. No more groggy zombies.

ONE 1-CUP SERVING

1 cucumber, peeled
½ honeydew melon or cantaloupe

1 Peel cucumber and juice it.

2 Scoop flesh out of melon, and juice the flesh only.

3 Stir the two fruit juices together thoroughly until dissolved in each other.

CALORIES	FAT	PROTEIN	SODIUM	CARBOHYDRATES	SUGARS	FIBER
76	0 grams	2 grams	21 milligrams	19 grams	12 grams	2 grams

NUTRITION NEWS: Water-Soluble Vitamin C

Essential vitamins are the vitamins we can only obtain through our diet. Fat-soluble vitamins, such as vitamins A, D, E, and K, can be stored in our bodies for a long period of time, but water-soluble vitamins, like vitamin C, cannot be stored and need to be eaten daily! One cup of cantaloupe has over 100 percent of the daily requirement for vitamin C. Drinking fresh juices with ingredients such as cantaloupe and cucumbers can help kids meet their daily need for vitamin C. Serving these vitamin C–rich juices first thing in the morning can put your mind at ease.

Apple Beeter Juice

Loads of nutrients are preserved when beets are juiced as opposed to when they are cooked. Drinking this beet juice gives kids energy and a variety of nutrients. When kids drink this juice, glucose from the fruit is easily absorbed into cells to become a primary energy source. Unused sugar gets stored as glycogen to be used for energy later.

TWO ½-CUP SERVINGS

1 beet, peeled and
   greens removed
2 red apples, cored

1 Place beet and apples into a juicer, and turn on.

2 Collect juice in a pitcher, and stir to combine.

CALORIES	FAT	PROTEIN	SODIUM	CARBOHYDRATES	SUGARS	FIBER
45	0 grams	1 gram	1 milligram	12 grams	9 grams	1 gram

MAKE IT FUN: Frozen Halloween Juice

For a scary Halloween drink, pour this red beet and apple juice mixture into a latex-free disposable glove. Tie the end of the glove to keep the juice from spilling out. Lay the juice-filled glove on a cookie sheet and place in the refrigerator. When the juice inside the glove is completely frozen through, cut off the latex glove from the frozen juice hand. Pop the red frozen juice hand into your punch bowl and add your favorite drinks. The kids will get quite a fright as they dip their ladles in the punch bowl to be surprised by the floating red hand!

Double Applenade

With antioxidants and vitamin C, this "double the apple juice" juice has the ability to keep kids healthy. Not only will it boost their immune systems, but it will also increase heart health and help keep their arteries clean.

TWO ½-CUP SERVINGS

2 red Gala apples, cored

1 Granny Smith apple, cored

¼ lemon, cut in half

1 Juice both types of apples and then the lemon, including the rind.

2 Collect into a pitcher and stir before serving.

CALORIES	FAT	PROTEIN	SODIUM	CARBOHYDRATES	SUGARS	FIBER
118	0 grams	1 gram	0 milligrams	31 grams	24 grams	3 grams

DIY: Applesauce

All kids have different texture preferences when it comes to food. Some kids like the feel of applesauce, some prefer crunchy raw apples, and others would rather have apple juice. Sometimes they decide to flip-flop between the three. Take advantage of any opportunities to get them to eat apples by serving all three types. Make your own applesauce without added sugar or preservatives. Slice an apple and remove the seeds. Chop the apple up into bite-sized pieces. Put apple chunks in a microwave-safe dish with 1–3 tablespoons of water. Cover and microwave on high for 1 minute. Take out and stir. Put back in microwave and heat again for 3–4 minutes. Take out and blend in a blender or food processor. Eat for breakfast!

Gimme a Beet!

A daily dose of beet juice can help kids retain their memory by increasing blood flow to the brain. Serve this juice up on the morning of a big test and give your kids an extra advantage.

TWO ½-CUP SERVINGS

2 oranges, peeled
1 beet, peeled and greens removed

1 Push orange and beet through a juicer as it's running.

2 Collect the juice into one container and stir.

CALORIES	FAT	PROTEIN	SODIUM	CARBOHYDRATES	SUGARS	FIBER
79	0 grams	2 grams	32 milligrams	19 grams	15 grams	4 grams

PICKY EATER: Gelatin Jigglers

One way kids love homemade juice is when it's used to replace water in Jell-O gelatin. Pour ¾ cup boiling water over 1 package of gelatin (4-serving size) and dissolve. Add 1 cup cold juice, like this beet-orange juice, and mix again until there is no gelatin left. Pour into a greased 8″ × 8″ cake pan and let chill in the fridge until firm, about 3 hours. Cut into it with a knife or cookie cutters and serve up on a tray.

Orange Pleaser Squeezers

Combining oranges, honeydew melon, and watermelon in this drink gives kids plenty of vitamin C for the day. School and playground viruses won't stand a chance in your home with a daily dose of this drink.

THREE ½-CUP SERVINGS

½ **honeydew melon, peeled**
½ **orange, peeled**
½ **cup watermelon, rind removed**

1 Combine all three fruits in the juicer, one after the other.

2 Juice all three fruits and collect in a single container. Stir before serving.

CALORIES	FAT	PROTEIN	SODIUM	CARBOHYDRATES	SUGARS	FIBER
77	0 grams	1 gram	30 milligrams	20 grams	17 grams	2 grams

PICKY EATER: Swiss Muesli

Enjoy this juice disguised as oatmeal. Swiss muesli is uncooked oatmeal soaked overnight in a liquid in the refrigerator. Start with 1 cup of rolled oats. Add 1 to 1½ cups juice to the oats, cover, and put in the fridge overnight. In the morning, add nuts, dried fruit, fresh fruit, or seeds. Mix the cold-soaked oats in the morning and enjoy.

Merry Melon

You can smell a cantaloupe even before cutting into it. The delicious fruity aroma will tempt kids on a weekend morning as they are trying to decide what they are hungry for. Once they smell the melon, they'll be craving this melon juice.

THREE ½-CUP SERVINGS

½ cantaloupe, rind removed

1 cup strawberries

1 Feed cantaloupe and strawberries through the funnel of a juicer, one after the other.

2 Collect the juice into a container and stir before serving.

CALORIES	FAT	PROTEIN	SODIUM	CARBOHYDRATES	SUGARS	FIBER
24	0 grams	1 gram	5 milligrams	6 grams	4 grams	1 gram

PICKY EATER: Using Juice for Syrup

Pancakes, waffles, and French toast all taste better with a little syrup on top. You can make your own syrup with no sugar added just by using some homemade juice. Take 2 cups of homemade juice, like the one in this recipe. Mix together 1 tablespoon cornstarch with 1 tablespoon cold water. Put juice and cornstarch in a saucepan on the stove. Bring juice to a boil over medium heat, for about 7–8 minutes, stirring continuously. Remove from heat and use it to top your pancakes or waffles. Although you can store it for several days in the fridge, you will want to warm it right before use, to prevent it from thickening up.

Kokomo Coconut

Let your kids escape to their own personal island oasis with this tropical coconut drink. This juice has all the makings to start a breezy summer day off just right—or to bring a little island paradise to a rainy fall day.

THREE ½-CUP SERVINGS

1 papaya, seeded
½ lime, peeled
1 cup unsweetened coconut milk

1 Juice the papaya and lime into a single pitcher.

2 Stir in the coconut milk until well combined.

CALORIES	FAT	PROTEIN	SODIUM	CARBOHYDRATES	SUGARS	FIBER
81	4 grams	1 gram	13 milligrams	12 grams	6 grams	2 grams

GREEN TIP: Using the Whole Coconut

Unlike many fruits, it is possible to use the entire coconut for different purposes. The coconut water can be poured out and used to drink. Athletes use this to hydrate because it's a natural way to balance electrolytes. The coconut flesh can be scooped out and grated for garnishing and flavorings and puréed into smoothies. The coconut flesh is also used to make coconut milk, as all the juice is squeezed from the coconut flesh itself. Lastly, recycle the coconut shells and use for tableware like bowls or cups. Decorate or paint it, fill it with soil, and use it as a flower pot. Fill it with wax and a wick and make candles.

Coolito Cranberry

Turn a mundane cereal breakfast into a fancy feast just by serving some homemade cranberry juice with your meal. Adding fruit juice helps kids to get a balanced meal and fill them up until lunch.

TWO ½-CUP SERVINGS

1¼ cups cranberries
2 red apples, cored

1 Juice the cranberries and apples into a single pitcher.

2 Stir the juices together until well combined.

CALORIES	FAT	PROTEIN	SODIUM	CARBOHYDRATES	SUGARS	FIBER
106	0 grams	1 gram	1 milligram	27 grams	21 grams	4 grams

TIME SAVER TIP: Batching

Batching refers to pairing similar tasks together and finishing those tasks before moving on to others. This is a great habit for busy families as it saves both time and energy. When preparing juices like this one, consider prepping all food for juicing right when you get home from the grocery store. Keep washed cranberries and cored apples in an airtight container in the fridge. Keep other fruit and vegetable juice combinations in separate containers. When you are ready to juice at a later time, this task will already be done and the mess cleaned up. You can then be ready for juicing this and other juices all at once, using your juicer and cleaning it only once.

White Whimsy Grape Fizzy

This grape juice has everything your kids love about grape juice, without the stains. When the kids inevitably spill their juice, you will not need to run to the rescue right away!

TWO ½-CUP SERVINGS

1½ cups green seedless grapes

2 limes, peeled

1 Put the grapes, then the lime, through the spout of a juicer and juice.

2 Combine both juices and stir thoroughly.

CALORIES	FAT	PROTEIN	SODIUM	CARBOHYDRATES	SUGARS	FIBER
98	0 grams	1 gram	4 milligrams	28 grams	19 grams	3 grams

DIY: Grape Juice Blends

Grape juice blends are popular on today's grocery store shelves. Your kids can customize their own blends by having juiced ice cubes of different fruits to drop in their grape juice. Begin with this recipe as your base. Have juice cubes available for add-ins such as cranberry juice cubes, apple juice cubes, lemon juice cubes, or pomegranate juice cubes. As the ice cubes slowly melt in their juice glass, they'll enjoy the blended flavors of the juices.

Carrot Top Garden Crop

Encourage your kids to drink carrot juices with a straw because otherwise they'll walk away with an orange mustache. Some kids just might want the orange mustache, though, so better ask them!

TWO ½-CUP SERVINGS

3 carrots
1 small banana, peeled
3 tablespoons water

1 Juice the carrots.

2 Place juice with the peeled banana in a blender until the mixture is smooth and runny.

3 Add water 1 tablespoon at a time until the juice is thin enough for your kids.

CALORIES	FAT	PROTEIN	SODIUM	CARBOHYDRATES	SUGARS	FIBER
96	0 grams	2 grams	75 milligrams	24 grams	12 grams	5 grams

DIY: Kids and Gardening

Growing your own carrots is not only a fun activity for kids, it's a great way to teach them where real food comes from. Kids who plant, care for, and harvest their own fruits and vegetables are more likely to eat those they grow, as well as other healthy fruits and vegetables. Carrots can be extra fun because they can get gnarly and crazy underground, rather than the typical pencil-shaped carrots kids are used to seeing. We once had a carrot that looked like a foot, complete with five "toes."

Oranchya Glad It's Morning

Kids are hungry when they first wake up. This juice is filling enough to satisfy them until you have time to pull yourself together, like getting dressed, before the chaos begins.

TWO ½-CUP SERVINGS

1 orange, split into segments

3 carrots

1 Juice the orange plus the carrots.

2 Stir together or shake in a cup that has a secure lid.

CALORIES	FAT	PROTEIN	SODIUM	CARBOHYDRATES	SUGARS	FIBER
75	0 grams	2 grams	75 milligrams	18 grams	11 grams	5 grams

NUTRITION NEWS: Choosing Oranges

Choosing oranges isn't difficult because they generally are picked when they are ripe and are available most of the year. Choosing the best oranges to juice, however, isn't as easy. The best oranges can be determined by the weight of the orange. The heavier the orange, the juicier it is. Bring your kids to the store and let them weigh an orange in each hand to determine which one is heavier. Then, let your children weigh the two oranges on a scale to see if they were right.

Beary Berry Blast

*With the shelf life of strawberries being so incredibly short,
you'll save money by juicing your uneaten strawberries
before they have a chance to go bad.*

FOUR ½-CUP SERVINGS

½ average cantaloupe
2 cups strawberries

1 Juice cantaloupe and strawberries together.

2 Stir thoroughly until the juice is well blended.

CALORIES	FAT	PROTEIN	SODIUM	CARBOHYDRATES	SUGARS	FIBER
23	0 grams	1 gram	6 milligrams	6 grams	4 grams	1 gram

GREEN TIP: The Dirty Dozen

Buying organic foods isn't always necessary when you are on a tight budget. However, there is a list of twelve fruits and vegetables, often called "The Dirty Dozen," that contain the highest amount of pesticides when grown commercially. If there is extra money in your budget for organic foods, these should be at the top of the list: apples, bell peppers, celery, cherries, grapes, lettuce, nectarines, peaches, pears, potatoes, spinach, and strawberries.

Dew Drop Drink

THREE ½-CUP SERVINGS

2 red Gala apples, cored
1½ cups strawberries
¼ lime, rind intact

1 Push apples, strawberries, and lime through the spout of a juicer and juice.

2 Collect in a single container and mix or stir before serving.

CALORIES	FAT	PROTEIN	SODIUM	CARBOHYDRATES	SUGARS	FIBER
76	0 grams	1 gram	1 milligram	20 grams	14 grams	3 grams

NUTRITION NEWS: Safe Food

Just because you wash your fruits and veggies when you get home doesn't always mean your kids are protected from food-borne illnesses. Produce recalls for foods like spinach and cantaloupe can be scary. The bacteria these foods can carry into your home can even be deadly. Stay safe by eating your fruits and veggies quickly after purchase. The longer they sit on a counter, the more time bacteria has to grow. For melons, wash and dry the skin. Cutting a wet melon may introduce bacteria into the flesh. Keep fruits and vegetables in the fridge at or below 40°F. This inhibits unnecessary bacteria growth. Don't fall into false security by purchasing organic produce. Although there may be no pesticides, there is a chance for germs. Make sure to check with *www.recall.gov* if you are unsure whether or not the food you have in your home has been recalled.

Cloudy with a Chance of Cucumbers

Although kids don't consider cucumbers a breakfast food, soon they'll be part of your mornings just like toast. Cucumbers start a day off well by adding some heart-healthy polyphenols, a special type of antioxidant responsible for controlling inflammation, to a child's diet.

ONE 1-CUP SERVING

1 cucumber, peeled
½ honeydew melon, rind removed
1 pear

1 Using a juicer, extract juice from the cucumber, melon, and pear.

2 Combine all juices in one container and stir.

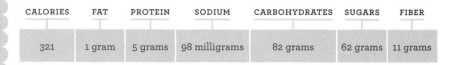

CALORIES	FAT	PROTEIN	SODIUM	CARBOHYDRATES	SUGARS	FIBER
321	1 gram	5 grams	98 milligrams	82 grams	62 grams	11 grams

GREEN TIP: Rinse Out Your Juicer

Maximizing the amount of juice your juicer is capable of producing is a great way to use all your resources. First, run your fruits and vegetables through your juicer and get as much juice as you can from your produce. Remove the extracted juice from the collection spout. Second, pour ½ cup of water into the intake funnel of your juicer, to rinse out any remaining juice you may have. This highly watered-down juice you can extract from your juicer contains vital nutrients that may have otherwise been washed down the drain. Use this diluted juice for athletes to drink, or include it in soups or sauces that call for water.

Prickly Pineapple

You'll want to keep some papaya in the freezer to make this juice even when papaya isn't in season. The tropical flavors will make your kids feel like it's summer, even in the dead of winter.

THREE ½-CUP SERVINGS

1 cup pineapple
½ orange
1 papaya, seeded

1 Juice the pineapple, orange, and the papaya into a single container.

2 Stir the juices from all three fruits thoroughly.

CALORIES	FAT	PROTEIN	SODIUM	CARBOHYDRATES	SUGARS	FIBER
77	0 grams	1 gram	4 milligrams	20 grams	13 grams	3 grams

DIY: Purchasing Pineapple

Purchasing a fresh pineapple is risky business, as it's hard to tell what's inside the thick skin. To choose a fresh pineapple, look for golden-colored skin on the base of the fruit and a sweet pineapple scent from the same area. The surface of the pineapple should give way slightly to pressure but still be firm. If you are still a little skeptical about the choice of pineapples, canned pineapple can be a great alternative and handles juicing well. Check the label to make sure there is no added sugar and the pineapple is canned in its own juice to keep your juice free of refined sugars.

Polka Dot Apricot

Dried apricots aren't the only way to enjoy this seasonal soft fruit. Freeze apricots when they are in season, with the pit removed, and you can enjoy this juice all year long.

TWO ½-CUP SERVINGS

4 apricots, pitted
2 Gala apples, peeled

1 Juice the apricots and apples into a container.

2 Stir before serving.

CALORIES	FAT	PROTEIN	SODIUM	CARBOHYDRATES	SUGARS	FIBER
110	0 grams	1 gram	1 milligram	28 grams	23 grams	3 grams

DIY: Drying Apricots

The apricot season is very short-lived. Once ripe on a tree, there is a very short window to harvest and eat the small fruit. However, apricots can be enjoyed all year long, and their dried counterparts make an excellent high-fiber snack. To dry them, simply wash and blot-dry fresh apricots. Then slice them down the middle to remove the pit. For a longer shelf life, and fresher taste, you may pre-treat the apricots with a solution of ascorbic acid, found in your local grocery store's canning section. Arrange on a dehydrator tray, or on a parchment-lined baking sheet. In a dehydrator, dry for 24–48 hours. In an oven at 150°F, and the door slightly ajar, allow to dry for 24–36 hours. When moisture is no longer in the apricot, yet the apricot is still pliable, it is finished.

Peachy Queen

The kids will want you to save some fresh grapes and peaches for this juice. Store a portion of the grapes and peaches in the refrigerator to ensure there are some left after snacking. In the fridge your fruit will last from 7-10 days, rather than 2-4 days on the counter.

THREE ½-CUP SERVINGS

2 peaches, pitted
1 cup red grapes
¼ lemon, peeled

1 Juice the peaches and grapes, and then the lemon.

2 Collect into a pitcher, and stir well before serving.

CALORIES	FAT	PROTEIN	SODIUM	CARBOHYDRATES	SUGARS	FIBER
74	0 grams	1 gram	1 milligram	19 grams	16 grams	2 grams

DIY: Quick After-School Snacks

Making your own after-school snacks is easy, smart, and cost-effective. Anytime you have fruits and vegetables out to prep for juicing, consider setting one or two of each fruit or veggie aside to prepare for snacks. Cleaning and cutting up fruit and veggies so they're ready to grab in the fridge means your kids are more likely to do so.

Carnival Carrot Cup

Always keep your fridge stocked with carrots for this delicious carrot-mango juice. Once mangoes are in season, grab a few and add them to your carrot juice for a breakfast juice full of vitamin A, vitamin C, and vitamin D for delicious!

TWO ½-CUP SERVINGS

3 carrots, peeled

1 mango, peeled and pitted

1 Put carrots and mango through a juicer, and juice.

2 Collect juice in a single cup, and stir.

CALORIES	FAT	PROTEIN	SODIUM	CARBOHYDRATES	SUGARS	FIBER
74	0 grams	1 gram	1 milligram	19 grams	16 grams	2 grams

PICKY EATER: Shredded Carrots

Carrots tend to be accepted by more children than any other vegetable (besides potatoes, of course). So take advantage of the fact kids like them. Use 3 carrots to make this juice, and take your remaining carrots and shred them. Make a salad using shredded carrots, raisins, and plain yogurt. Add shredded carrots to muffins, cookies, or cakes. Use shredded carrots for soups and stews. Chop carrots and serve with a dip, such as ranch. Best of all, the hearty nature of carrots makes them a perfect on-the-go snack! Take them raw anytime you need to bring a snack somewhere!

Sunshine Strapple

*Room temperature apple juice isn't too satisfying to kids
(or adults, either!). Keep the juice in the fridge, or even freezer,
to keep it chilled. You could also serve apple juice warmed
with a little cinnamon added for an apple-spice drink.*

TWO ½-CUP SERVINGS

1 apple, cored

1 cup strawberries,
  hulls intact

1 Juice the apple and then the strawberries into a single container.

2 Stir the juices together, and serve over ice.

CALORIES	FAT	PROTEIN	SODIUM	CARBOHYDRATES	SUGARS	FIBER
62	0 grams	1 gram	1 milligram	16 grams	12 grams	3 grams

PICKY EATER: Keep Apple Juice Clear

If there is one thing kids seem loath to drink, it's brown, thick, or cloudy apple juice. One way to keep your apple juice from turning brown is to feed a slice of lemon into your juicer just before juicing your apples. The ascorbic acid in the lemon will keep the apple juice looking fresh. To filter apple juice to make it look less cloudy, simply pour it through a coffee filter until the juice is clearer.

Sour Grapple

Drink this grape-apple-lemon juice with an egg, cheese, and lettuce sandwich for breakfast. A breakfast with whole grains, protein, dairy, veggies, and fruit is a great way to start the day.

THREE ½-CUP SERVINGS

1 cup red grapes
1 apple, cored
½ lemon, peeled

1 Juice the grapes, apple, and lemon into one container.

2 Stir juices together so they are thoroughly mixed. Serve.

CALORIES	FAT	PROTEIN	SODIUM	CARBOHYDRATES	SUGARS	FIBER
63	0 grams	1 gram	1 milligram	17 grams	13 grams	1 gram

MAKE IT FUN: Invisible Writing

Teach your kids a chemistry lesson, use up the lemon juice, and have fun while you're doing it. Juice the other half of your lemon and put the juice in a small bowl. Use paintbrushes to paint lemon juice onto a piece of paper into shapes, letters, or pictures. Let the paper dry. Hold the paper up to a light bulb until the paper heats up. The picture painted by the lemon juice will darken and the image will become visible. The acid in the lemon weakens the paper and turns brown when heated. Try other fruit juices and see what different colors you can make!

Moonlight Mango

Dark, cold winter mornings can be a drag for kids. Brighten up their morning with this sunshiny, tasty, island pineapple-mango juice. The kids will feel revived and rejuvenated and ready to tackle the day.

FOUR ½-CUP SERVINGS

1 cup pineapple, peeled and cut into chunks

1 mango, pitted

1 cucumber, peeled

½ lemon with the rind

1 Push the pineapple, mango, cucumber, and lemon through the spout of a juicer, one at a time.

2 Collect the juice into one container. Stir and swirl to combine the juices thoroughly.

CALORIES	FAT	PROTEIN	SODIUM	CARBOHYDRATES	SUGARS	FIBER
67	0 grams	1 gram	3 milligrams	18 grams	13 grams	2 grams

PICKY EATER: Let Them Dip!

Kids love eating finger food when they can use it to scoop dips! Whether they are eating fruits, vegetables, chips, or breads, prepare some healthy homemade dips for them to eat with. Fruit juices, like this one, can be added to fruit dips for a powerful flavor pop. Start with 8 ounces softened light cream cheese. Add 1 tablespoon powdered sugar and ¼ cup fresh homemade juice. Beat together with beaters until well incorporated.

3

Ready for Anything:

DRINKS ON THE GO

Have you ever stopped at the end of the day to realize you and your kids had been gone the whole day? With soccer games, gymnastics, school, church groups, or just running errands, we spend a lot of time outside of the house and in our cars. We also eat on the go.

Instead of heading to a fast-food restaurant when the kids start to get cranky, plan ahead! Bring smoothies and juices on your travels to keep kids' blood sugar steady, keep your sanity, and fill nutrition gaps during the day.

Smoothies and juices brought to games help young athletes play their best game. Kids who eat fries and soda before a soccer game have little energy to make it through an hour of play time. Kids who are fueled with fruits and vegetables have more energy and play harder, stronger, and longer.

When bringing these drinks on errands or on your morning commute, make sure you use cups that are properly sealed to prevent spilling and that are properly insulated to keep the beverage cold. You can freeze cups ahead of time to help keep juices and smoothies cold. Your kids will be more pleasant, healthier, and happier as you phase out the trips to the fast-food restaurants and replace them with wholesome drinks and snacks.

Carrot Blitz Smoothie

Coconut milk is a great base for this smoothie and perfect for athletes who want to stay hydrated. Load up on coconut milk and make different variations of this smoothie depending on what fruit is in season. Peaches, apricots, apples, or oranges can all replace the banana in this drink, depending on the time of year.

FOUR ½-CUP SERVINGS

½ cup romaine lettuce
2 carrots, peeled
2 bananas, peeled
½ cup coconut milk

1 Place romaine lettuce, carrots, bananas, and coconut milk into a blender.

2 Blend until all fruit and vegetables are smooth and no longer chunky.

CALORIES	FAT	PROTEIN	SODIUM	CARBOHYDRATES	SUGARS	FIBER
82	2 grams	1 gram	30 milligrams	17 grams	9 grams	3 grams

NUTRITION NEWS: Hydration and Athletic Performance

Proper hydration is essential to athletic performance. The sodium-potassium balance is key to maintaining this hydration. Bananas and coconut milk contain the right amount of potassium and sodium to keep cells in balance and allow kids to maximize their potential on the field, without filling up on artificially flavored and artificially colored sports drinks.

Merry Fairies Triple Berries

This smoothie is especially quick to make! There is no chopping, seeding, or peeling any of the ingredients. Just throw in a blender and go!

FOUR 1-CUP SERVINGS

1 cup romaine lettuce
1 cup blackberries, frozen
1 cup strawberries, frozen
1 cup blueberries, frozen
1 cup 100-percent pure
   orange juice

1 Place lettuce, berries, and ½ cup orange juice in a blender, and blend until smooth.

2 Add remaining juice, and blend until smoothie is desired consistency.

CALORIES	FAT	PROTEIN	SODIUM	CARBOHYDRATES	SUGARS	FIBER
94	1 gram	2 grams	6 milligrams	21 grams	12 grams	5 grams

NUTRITION NEWS: Blueberries

Super-high in antioxidants and nutrients, blueberries are considered a super-food. Anthocyanins are powerful antioxidants that control free radical damage. Consuming anthocyanins may help protect our kids from cancer, inflammation, bacterial infections, and diabetes. While other blue or purple fruits also contain this antioxidant, blueberries are a delicious source.

Yam Kablam!

This smoothie is concentrated with energy from the sweet potatoes or yams. If you're headed to a Little League game, or just out for a long morning of errands, this smoothie will give kids a boost and leave behind the groggy.

FOUR 1-CUP SERVINGS

2 sweet potatoes or yams, either leftover baked with the flesh scooped out, or raw and peeled and chopped finely

2 cups vanilla soy milk

1 teaspoon ground cloves

1 teaspoon ground cinnamon

½" knob of ginger

1 cup baby spinach leaves

1 Put sweet potatoes or yams into blender. Add 1 cup soy milk.

2 Blend until smooth, and then add cloves, cinnamon, ginger, and spinach.

3 Add remaining 1 cup soy milk, and blend until smooth.

CALORIES	FAT	PROTEIN	SODIUM	CARBOHYDRATES	SUGARS	FIBER
63	0 grams	1 gram	44 milligrams	15 grams	3 grams	3 grams

TIME SAVER TIP: Saving Ginger

Fresh ginger is great to have around. The flavor you can get from freshly grated ginger is much stronger than dried ginger stored in your spice rack. There is no reason to run out and buy a fresh chunk of ginger anytime you are ready to use it. Ginger can be stored nicely in the fridge or freezer, in a simple zip-top bag. When you are ready to use it, simply grate off some from the end and return to the fridge. Choose gingerroots that have thick skin and look mature. Thick-skinned ginger has the best flavor!

Grapeology

Store grapes in the freezer for this smoothie, and you'll always have the ingredients you need. Kids will love throwing a few frozen grapes into the blender, then sneaking a few into their mouths.

FOUR 1-CUP SERVINGS

1 cup Belgian endive
2 cups red grapes
2 pears, cored
1 banana, peeled
1 cup grape juice

1 Take Belgian endive, grapes, pears, banana, and ½ cup juice, and place in blender. Turn blender on, and mix until combined.

2 Add remaining juice, and turn the blender on again until smooth and well mixed.

CALORIES	FAT	PROTEIN	SODIUM	CARBOHYDRATES	SUGARS	FIBER
138	0 grams	2 grams	5 milligrams	35 grams	27 grams	4 grams

PICKY EATER: Decorate with Food

The grapes in this smoothie make beautiful garnishing for the drink itself. Skewer the grapes on a wooden stick, alternating with green and red grapes if you have them. Use skewered grapes as a stirring stick for the drink. Another idea is to skewer the grapes onto a straw for a decorative straw.

Magical Melon Mix

Send this smoothie to school in your children's lunch box in a well-insulated Thermos or drink container. Start with it frozen, and by lunchtime the smoothie will be defrosted and ready to drink.

FOUR 1-CUP SERVINGS

1 cup kale

2 cucumber, peeled

½ cantaloupe, rind and seeds removed

1 pear, cored

1 banana, peeled

2 cups orange juice

1 Take kale, cucumber, cantaloupe, pear, banana, and 1 cup orange juice, and place in blender. Blend until smooth and well incorporated.

2 Add remaining 1 cup orange juice, and blend until smooth.

CALORIES	FAT	PROTEIN	SODIUM	CARBOHYDRATES	SUGARS	FIBER
128	1 gram	2 grams	21 milligrams	31 grams	21 grams	3 grams

DIY: Buying Kale

If you haven't had a chance to shop for kale at the grocery store before, don't worry—it's not that scary! You've probably walked right past it, not knowing what it is. Kale is usually found in the produce department close to other green leafy vegetables like spinach, green leaf lettuce, and romaine. Check the label on the tie holding the leaves together to make sure you are picking up kale. The leaves are very curly and a deep, dark green. Avoid purchasing kale where the leaves look yellow, dry, or wilted.

Monster Mango Mash

*Freeze this smoothie, then take it with you. By the time it defrosts,
your kids will be hungry and ready for a treat. Bring along some
nuts to eat, and they'll feel like they just had lunch.*

FOUR 1-CUP SERVINGS

1 cup spinach

2 mangoes, pitted and
   peeled

2 pints raspberries

1 teaspoon vanilla
   extract

1½ cups coconut milk

1 Add all ingredients to blender.

2 Blend until smooth. Add more coconut milk
if necessary until spinach is completely
undetectable.

CALORIES	FAT	PROTEIN	SODIUM	CARBOHYDRATES	SUGARS	FIBER
178	5 grams	2 grams	20 milligrams	34 grams	21 grams	10 grams

DIY: Choosing a Mango

According to the National Mango Board, the biggest misconception is that a
mango's ripeness depends on its color. This is not true. Mango colors range
from red to yellow to green. The best way to choose a mango is to give it a
gentle squeeze. If it is soft to the squeeze, it will be ripe. A ripe mango will
also smell fruity by the stem. You can use this same technique when choosing
avocados and peaches.

Pucker Up Peach

Watercress is high in iron and folate, two minerals many kids are lacking in these days. Watercress gives a new flavor to this smoothie, but it may be hard to find. If you can't find watercress at your grocery store, you can also substitute arugula, radicchio, or spinach.

FOUR 1-CUP SERVINGS

1 cup watercress
1 orange, peeled
2 peaches, pitted
1 banana, peeled
1 cup coconut milk

1 Combine watercress, orange, peaches, banana, and ½ cup coconut milk. Blend on high.

2 Continue to add the rest of the coconut milk until smoothie is no longer chunky.

CALORIES	FAT	PROTEIN	SODIUM	CARBOHYDRATES	SUGARS	FIBER
99	3 grams	1 gram	11 milligrams	18 grams	13 grams	3 grams

TIME SAVER TIP: Prepare and Store

Prepare your produce for your smoothie and portion into containers for easier smoothie-making mornings. For this recipe, peel and section an orange, chop 1 cup watercress, slice and pit 2 peaches, and peel and cut a banana. Place all fruits and the vegetable into a covered dish in the fridge or a zip-top storage bag. In the morning, dump the entire bowl or container into blender and add the liquid. No mess and no dishes!

Dandy Lions and Happy Kids

Although bitter when eaten raw, the dandelion greens here lose their bitterness to the pineapple. Lemon or sugar can also help cut the bitterness of greens, making them more pleasant for your little ones to eat.

FOUR 1-CUP SERVINGS

½ cup dandelion greens
½ cup arugula
2 cups pineapple, peeled and cored
1 banana, peeled
2 cups coconut milk

1 Combine the dandelion greens, arugula, pineapple, and banana in a blender.

2 Pour 1 cup coconut milk in blender, and blend until smooth.

3 Pour the remaining coconut milk into the blender, and continue to blend until all ingredients are well incorporated.

CALORIES	FAT	PROTEIN	SODIUM	CARBOHYDRATES	SUGARS	FIBER
124	6 grams	1 gram	16 milligrams	19 grams	12 grams	2 grams

PICKY EATER: Make Enough for Everyone

When preparing these smoothies, make enough for everyone to have some, including Mom and Dad. Sending the message that only the kids need to drink healthy smoothies will almost always be met with resistance. The message to send to kids is that healthy food is good for everyone in the family, not just the parent with high cholesterol or the teenager trying to lose weight. Everyone benefits, so everyone should be drinking! If you want your picky eater to drink up, drink yourselves.

Celerapple Frapple

Wrap celery in foil and store in the freezer. Your celery will last longer, and you'll always have some on hand when you are ready to make this smoothie.

FOUR 1-CUP SERVINGS

1 cup romaine lettuce
3 Granny Smith apples, peeled and cored
2 celery stalks
2 cups orange juice

1 Combine lettuce, apples, celery, and 1 cup juice into blender, and blend until smooth.

2 Add remaining 1 cup juice, and continue to blend until smoothie reaches desired consistency.

CALORIES	FAT	PROTEIN	SODIUM	CARBOHYDRATES	SUGARS	FIBER
124	0 grams	1 gram	19 milligrams	31 grams	23 grams	3 grams

Simple Raw Applesauce

Applesauce from the store is not as fresh as homemade and often comes with fillers, sugar, and preservatives. Making your own applesauce is as easy as making your own smoothies. Slice your apples to fit into a good blender. Use your blender's tamper to push the apples onto the blade while it's processing. Blend until texture of chunky applesauce. Serve right away as the applesauce will turn brown. Add cinnamon for extra flavor! Use some of your fresh applesauce for this smoothie.

Moonberry Mug

Squeeze your own orange juice, or have some 100-percent pure orange juice on hand for this delicious drink. Have it ready when your kids walk in the door after a long day at school.

FOUR 1-CUP SERVINGS

1 cup spinach
2 cups blueberries
1 cup blackberries
1 tablespoon flax meal
2 cups orange juice

1 Place spinach, blueberries, blackberries, flax meal, and 1 cup orange juice in a blender, and turn on.

2 Slowly add as much of the orange juice as necessary, while the blender is mixing, until the smoothie is the consistency you desire.

CALORIES	FAT	PROTEIN	SODIUM	CARBOHYDRATES	SUGARS	FIBER
139	2 grams	3 grams	15 milligrams	29 grams	18 grams	4 grams

GREEN TIP: Stretching Your Spinach

When purchasing produce, getting as much life out of it as possible is a great way to save money and the environment. Spinach is a fragile vegetable that should be properly stored to get the most life from it. Start with spinach that is bright green, with no signs of yellowing. Any spinach leaves that have a slimy coating or look damaged, bruised, or bent will not last very long in your home. Do not wash the spinach until you are ready to use it. This will accelerate the decay of the leaves. Store in a plastic bag, with as much of the air squeezed out of it as possible. Place in the fridge for up to five days, no longer.

Oh, Nuts!

Almonds pack protein and healthy fats, both of which are found to be satiating. This smoothie will fill up little tummies, curb major mood swings, and prevent dramatic dips in blood sugar.

FOUR 1-CUP SERVINGS

¼ cup almonds
¾ cup water
1 cup romaine lettuce
1 apple, peeled and cored
1 banana, peeled
1 cup Greek-style yogurt

1 Combine almonds and water in blender and blend until creamy.

2 Add romaine lettuce, apple, banana, and ½ cup yogurt. Blend again until creamy.

3 Add the last ½ cup yogurt, and blend until desired consistency is achieved.

CALORIES	FAT	PROTEIN	SODIUM	CARBOHYDRATES	SUGARS	FIBER
115	3 grams	8 grams	26 milligrams	16 grams	10 grams	2 grams

TIME SAVER TIP: Ready-to-Go Bananas

Bananas have a very short shelf life. Sometimes it feels like the turn from yellow to brown happens overnight. When a banana goes soft, toss the whole banana, peel and all, into the freezer. When you are ready to make this smoothie, or other recipes that call for a banana, take the banana out of the freezer. Let it soften for about 5 minutes, and then peel. Throw the banana into the blender for a quick smoothie.

Brainy Bananarama

*Recruit the kids to help in making this drink. Bananas
and clementines can be peeled by most children.
The rest of the ingredients don't need to be cut at all.*

FOUR 1-CUP SERVINGS

1 cup spinach
1 banana, peeled
1 cup strawberries
1 cup blueberries
1 cup blackberries
2 clementines or
   tangerines
1 cup water

1 Combine spinach, banana, strawberries, blueberries, blackberries, clementines, and ½ cup
water in a high-powered blender, and blend.

2 Continue to blend, and add the remaining
½ cup water until drink is smooth.

CALORIES	FAT	PROTEIN	SODIUM	CARBOHYDRATES	SUGARS	FIBER
73	1 gram	1 gram	10 milligrams	17 grams	9 grams	3 grams

PICKY EATER: Engage the Kids in the Kitchen

Teaching kids to learn their way around the kitchen can never be started too
soon. From the moment they can pick up a spoon, drop food into a blender, or
flip a switch, they can be part of meal prep. Smoothies are the perfect beginning for young chefs. They can learn to follow a recipe, prepare the drinks, and
serve them to the family. Kids are so proud of accomplishments such as these
and are generally anxious to try their own creations.

Forget Me Not, Apricot

After an apricot harvest, save some apricots for this smoothie, eat some fresh, dry some, and freeze the rest. You'll always be ready for Forget Me Not, Apricot all year long.

FOUR 1-CUP SERVINGS

1 cup romaine lettuce

3 apricots

2 bananas, peeled

2 cups water

1 Combine romaine, apricots, bananas, and 1 cup water in a blender, and blend as well as you can, about 30 seconds.

2 Add the remaining 1 cup water, and blend until smoothie is desired consistency.

CALORIES	FAT	PROTEIN	SODIUM	CARBOHYDRATES	SUGARS	FIBER
67	0 grams	1 gram	2 milligrams	17 grams	10 grams	2 grams

NUTRITION NEWS: Apricots

Apricots are an amazing fruit to include in your kids' diet. As an excellent source of vitamin A, apricots can help with good vision and protect the eyes from damage. Apricots are also a good source of potassium, which is great for fluid balance when kids are playing in the hot summer. Apricots are also a source of tryptophan, helping kids sleep after a long, hard day.

The Duke's Cuke

Including grapefruit in smoothies like this one helps busy kids fight colds they don't have time to fight. Kids won't have to miss school or practice when they don't get sick.

FOUR 1-CUP SERVINGS

1 cup watercress
1 pink grapefruit, peeled
2 cucumbers, peeled
2 cups orange juice

1 Place watercress, grapefruit, cucumbers, and 1 cup orange juice in a blender, and blend for 30 seconds on low.

2 Add remaining 1 cup orange juice, and continue to blend until smoothie is desired consistency.

CALORIES	FAT	PROTEIN	SODIUM	CARBOHYDRATES	SUGARS	FIBER
44	0 grams	2 grams	6 milligrams	11 grams	7 grams	1 gram

TIME SAVER TIP: Organize the Kitchen

Looking for lost items is a huge waste of time. Have you tried digging through a junk drawer looking for your vegetable peeler, or scouring the cabinets searching for the blender lid? What could be a 3-minute smoothie-making event suddenly becomes 30 minutes. When you need to get out the door in a jiffy, make sure your kitchen is organized. Keep blender parts together in a convenient spot. Keep vegetable peelers in a sorted drawer close to where you will use it. Having things where you can find them again is a huge time saver.

Peter Piper's Pumpkin Smoothie

The spiced flavor of this smoothie helps disguise the full cup of spinach. Your kids will be surprised at how similar this smoothie is to pumpkin pie. Break out the whipped topping!

FOUR 1-CUP SERVINGS

1 cup spinach

2 raw sweet potatoes, peeled and chopped

1 teaspoon cinnamon

1 teaspoon pumpkin pie spice

2 cups almond milk

1 cup ice

1 Combine spinach, sweet potatoes, cinnamon, pumpkin pie spice, and 1 cup almond milk. Turn blender on high, and mix to combine, about 30 seconds.

2 Add remaining 1 cup almond milk and ice, and blend again until smoothie is desired consistency.

CALORIES	FAT	PROTEIN	SODIUM	CARBOHYDRATES	SUGARS	FIBER
123	2 grams	5 grams	103 milligrams	21 grams	8 grams	3 grams

DIY: Pumpkin Pie Spice

Spices come in so many combinations, it's almost impossible to own all of them. You can make your own, however, when you find yourself with a recipe that calls for a combo spice and you don't have that one in your cupboard. For pumpkin pie spice, use 1 teaspoon ground cinnamon, ½ teaspoon ground ginger, ¼ teaspoon nutmeg, and ¼ teaspoon allspice. Store the pumpkin pie spice in an airtight container until ready to use.

Sweet Lemon Treat

Summertime and lemonade go hand in hand, but lemonade is loaded with sugar. Start a new tradition of summertime and lemon smoothies, and your kids will be well hydrated with less sugar.

FOUR 1-CUP SERVINGS

2 apples, peeled and cored

4 lemons, peeled

1 tablespoon honey

2 cups water

1 cup ice

1 Combine apple, lemons, honey, and 1 cup water in a blender, and blend for 30 seconds.

2 Add the remaining 1 cup water and ice, and blend until smooth and thoroughly mixed.

CALORIES	FAT	PROTEIN	SODIUM	CARBOHYDRATES	SUGARS	FIBER
71	0 grams	1 gram	1 milligram	20 grams	14 grams	3 grams

NUTRITION NEWS: Honey

Even though honey is sweeter, it is actually better for your kids than table sugar. Honey contains vitamins and minerals such as vitamin B, magnesium, potassium, and calcium. Table sugar has been stripped of its nutrients. The enzymes in table sugar are mostly destroyed, while honey keeps its enzymes. Lastly, honey is less likely to spike blood sugar because it is absorbed more slowly into the bloodstream. Honey has also been shown to have a soothing effect on sore throats. So, next time you have a choice, choose honey.

Tambourines and Tangerines

When your kids have to accompany you on your morning commute, you'll be glad you brought along this tropical smoothie. The soothing tastes of the tropics will help all of you to forget you are actually in Monday-morning traffic.

FOUR 1-CUP SERVINGS

1 cup watercress
2 grapefruits, peeled
2 clementines or
   tangerines
1 cup pineapple
1 tablespoon honey
1 cup water
1 cup ice

1 Place watercress, grapefruits, clementines, pineapple, honey, and ½ cup water in a blender, and blend for 30 seconds, making sure all the food is pushed onto the blades.

2 Continue to blend while adding the remaining ½ cup water and ice. Blend until it reaches desired consistency.

CALORIES	FAT	PROTEIN	SODIUM	CARBOHYDRATES	SUGARS	FIBER
79	0 grams	1 gram	4 milligrams	20 grams	17 grams	2 grams

GREEN TIP: Use Less Energy with Smoothies

Make your carbon footprint smaller by cooking less. The more time you spend using the stove and oven, the more energy you use. Smoothies are great for a quick meal that doesn't require much energy use. Use even less energy by helping your blender out. When you chop your food sufficiently and add more water, the blender can blend up a smoothie with less effort.

Alexander the Grape

Taking pears to school for lunch has never worked well.
They get beat up and bruised by the time your kids get to class.
For kids who love pears, send along this pear-and-grape
smoothie in their lunch instead with an ice pack to keep it cold.

FOUR 1-CUP SERVINGS

1 cup iceberg lettuce
3 cups green grapes
2 pears, cored and
    peeled
1 cup almond milk
1 cup ice

1 Place lettuce, grapes, pears, and almond milk in a blender, and blend until smooth.

2 Add the ice, and blend until desired consistency.

CALORIES	FAT	PROTEIN	SODIUM	CARBOHYDRATES	SUGARS	FIBER
130	1 gram	3 grams	35 milligrams	29 grams	23 grams	3 grams

MAKE IT FUN: Use Small Cups

Often parents' eyes are much bigger than our kids' stomachs. Keep portions on the small side. To make drinking this smoothie extra-fun though, consider tiny glasses such as play tea cups or shot glasses. Kids can drink up their smoothie in one gulp. Then pour them some more. They'll feel like they are drinking more than they are and love the feedback of "finishing" their drinks.

Citrus Squeezer Teaser

"Creamy" and "thirst-quenching" aren't often used in the same description, but this smoothie is an exception. The citrus satisfies thirst, while the yogurt adds the creaminess of ice cream, similar to sorbet.

FOUR 1-CUP SERVINGS

1 cup kale
3 cups pineapple
1 clementine, peeled
½ lemon, peeled
1 cup vanilla yogurt
1 cup ice

1 Combine all ingredients but ice in a blender, and blend at a high speed until combined.

2 Add the ice, and blend until the texture is desired.

CALORIES	FAT	PROTEIN	SODIUM	CARBOHYDRATES	SUGARS	FIBER
139	1 gram	5 grams	50 milligrams	31 grams	24 grams	3 grams

MAKE IT FUN: Shaped Ice Cubes

With a myriad of fun-shaped ice cube trays on the market, ice will never be boring again. Dolphins, hearts, flowers, stars, and more can turn water into ice kids will want to add to their smoothies, homemade juices, and glasses of water. Pour your smoothies or homemade juices into the shaped ice cube trays, and use those cubes to mix and match smoothies of different flavors and foods.

Peaches and Dreams

Stopping for a drink or treat on the road means having something that will almost always be served with added sugar. Bring this sweet drink instead. It has no sugar added and tastes so much better.

FOUR 1-CUP SERVINGS

1 cup romaine lettuce
3 peaches, pitted
2 bananas, peeled
1 cup vanilla kefir
1 cup ice

1 Place all ingredients except ice in a blender. Blend until smooth.

2 Add ice and blend until texture is smooth.

CALORIES	FAT	PROTEIN	SODIUM	CARBOHYDRATES	SUGARS	FIBER
131	1 gram	5 grams	49 milligrams	29 grams	21 grams	3 grams

NUTRITION NEWS: Kefir Versus Yogurt

This smoothie (as well as the others) can be made using kefir or yogurt. Kefir and yogurt are very similar and can be used interchangeably in many recipes. They both are usually made from cow's milk. They are both good sources of calcium, phosphorus, magnesium, and vitamin D. They are both similar in texture, with kefir being a little more gelatin-like. They are pretty close in taste, with kefir a little more tart. They both contain beneficial live bacteria, although kefir has been shown to have about five times more strains of beneficial bacteria than yogurt.

Nuttin' Honey

When you need something filling on the road to tide your kids over until a very late meal, bring along this smoothie. The protein and fat in the nuts have been shown to be more satiating than carbohydrates and sugars.

FOUR 1-CUP SERVINGS

⅓ cup walnuts
⅓ cup almonds
1 tablespoon ground
    flaxseed
2 cups almond milk
2 bananas, peeled
1½ tablespoons honey
    or agave nectar
1 cup ice

1 Combine walnuts, almonds, flaxseed, and 1 cup almond milk in a blender, and blend until nuts are mostly ground, just before turning to a paste.

2 Add the remaining 1 cup almond milk, bananas, and honey or agave, and blend until smooth.

3 Add ice, and blend one more time until smoothie is desired consistency.

CALORIES	FAT	PROTEIN	SODIUM	CARBOHYDRATES	SUGARS	FIBER
192	7 grams	6 grams	63 milligrams	29 grams	19 grams	3 grams

NUTRITION NEWS: *Walnuts*

Major research is currently being conducted on the health benefits of walnuts. Many of these benefits are found in the skin of the walnuts. The skin contains more than 90 percent of the total phenols, an organic compound with antioxidant properties, in a walnut. Walnuts are also high in vitamin E and omega-3 fatty acids, both of which are good for kids' skin. Smoothies are a great place to include the sometimes bitter taste of the walnut skin. Blending it up into a smoothie and adding the sweetness of the fruits makes it easier to eat and get the benefits from the whole nut.

Tropical Pineapple Punch

With lemons, limes, grapefruit, pineapple, and oranges all in one drink, the vitamin C in this smoothie is unmatched. These citrus fruits are perfect for bringing this smoothie on the go, as the acid in citrus foods acts as a natural preservative.

FOUR 1-CUP SERVINGS

2 large kale leaves
1 cup pineapple, peeled and cubed
1 large orange, peeled
1 grapefruit, peeled
½ lemon, peeled
½ lime, peeled

1 Combine all ingredients in a blender in the order listed.

2 Blend until desired consistency.

CALORIES	FAT	PROTEIN	SODIUM	CARBOHYDRATES	SUGARS	FIBER
68	0 grams	2 grams	7 milligrams	17 grams	12 grams	3 grams

PICKY EATER: Eating Lemons

Even babies pucker up from the sour taste of lemons, yet many kids love lemonade. Lemons don't need to be eaten alone to get their benefits, and often combining them with other foods is the most pleasing way to eat them. Add lemon to drinks, smoothies, salads, pancakes, ice cream, custards, or even water. Just remember, the white pith, just beneath the skin, is bitter, so remove as much of this as possible.

Nuttin' Honey

When you need something filling on the road to tide your kids over until a very late meal, bring along this smoothie. The protein and fat in the nuts have been shown to be more satiating than carbohydrates and sugars.

FOUR 1-CUP SERVINGS

⬚ cup walnuts
⬚ cup almonds
1 tablespoon ground
  flaxseed
2 cups almond milk
2 bananas, peeled
1½ tablespoons honey
  or agave nectar
1 cup ice

1 Combine walnuts, almonds, flaxseed, and 1 cup almond milk in a blender, and blend until nuts are mostly ground, just before turning to a paste.

2 Add the remaining 1 cup almond milk, bananas, and honey or agave, and blend until smooth.

3 Add ice, and blend one more time until smoothie is desired consistency.

CALORIES	FAT	PROTEIN	SODIUM	CARBOHYDRATES	SUGARS	FIBER
192	7 grams	6 grams	63 milligrams	29 grams	19 grams	3 grams

NUTRITION NEWS: Walnuts

Major research is currently being conducted on the health benefits of walnuts. Many of these benefits are found in the skin of the walnuts. The skin contains more than 90 percent of the total phenols, an organic compound with antioxidant properties, in a walnut. Walnuts are also high in vitamin E and omega-3 fatty acids, both of which are good for kids' skin. Smoothies are a great place to include the sometimes bitter taste of the walnut skin. Blending it up into a smoothie and adding the sweetness of the fruits makes it easier to eat and get the benefits from the whole nut.

Tropical Pineapple Punch

With lemons, limes, grapefruit, pineapple, and oranges all in one drink, the vitamin C in this smoothie is unmatched. These citrus fruits are perfect for bringing this smoothie on the go, as the acid in citrus foods acts as a natural preservative.

FOUR 1-CUP SERVINGS

2 large kale leaves

1 cup pineapple, peeled and cubed

1 large orange, peeled

1 grapefruit, peeled

½ lemon, peeled

½ lime, peeled

1 Combine all ingredients in a blender in the order listed.

2 Blend until desired consistency.

CALORIES	FAT	PROTEIN	SODIUM	CARBOHYDRATES	SUGARS	FIBER
68	0 grams	2 grams	7 milligrams	17 grams	12 grams	3 grams

PICKY EATER: Eating Lemons

Even babies pucker up from the sour taste of lemons, yet many kids love lemonade. Lemons don't need to be eaten alone to get their benefits, and often combining them with other foods is the most pleasing way to eat them. Add lemon to drinks, smoothies, salads, pancakes, ice cream, custards, or even water. Just remember, the white pith, just beneath the skin, is bitter, so remove as much of this as possible.

Luscious Lemon-Lime

*Replace the lemon-lime soda that has parked itself in the
backseat cup holder of your car with this healthy lemon-lime
smoothie. The vitamins and minerals are a welcome
change from the sugar and empty calories.*

FOUR 1-CUP SERVINGS

1 cup romaine lettuce
2 lemons, peeled
2 limes, peeled
½ cup kefir
1 tablespoon agave
   nectar

1 Combine romaine lettuce, lemons, limes, and
kefir, and blend until thoroughly combined.

2 Add agave nectar, and blend until desired texture is achieved.

CALORIES	FAT	PROTEIN	SODIUM	CARBOHYDRATES	SUGARS	FIBER
54	0 grams	2 grams	26 milligrams	13 grams	8 grams	2 grams

NUTRITION NEWS: Soda Warnings

Soda is high in calories and completely void of nutrients. These empty calories
lead to overeating in children who are starving for nutrients. Chemicals and preservatives added to soda lead to bone loss and poor bone development. Kids
who drink soda do not drink adequate amounts of water each day, because
soda is taking the place of water. The acid in sodas can lead to inflammation
of the digestive tract and can be painful for sensitive stomachs. For these reasons, it makes sense to teach your kids to avoid sodas. Send them out with a
smoothie instead, and none of these problems are an issue.

Crashing Coconut Coolers

When taking these coconut coolers on the road, bring along
cups with lids that won't fall off. Throw some ice in the cup,
and this coconut drink will stay cold until it's gone.

FOUR 1-CUP SERVINGS

1 cup romaine lettuce
Flesh of 2 coconuts
1 tablespoon lemon
　juice
1 banana, peeled
¼" ginger, peeled
½ cup almond milk
½ cup plain yogurt

1 Place romaine, coconut flesh, lemon juice, banana, ginger, and almond milk in a blender and blend.

2 Add yogurt, and blend until desired smoothie consistency is achieved.

CALORIES	FAT	PROTEIN	SODIUM	CARBOHYDRATES	SUGARS	FIBER
54	0 grams	2 grams	26 milligrams	13 grams	8 grams	2 grams

TIME SAVER TIP: Eating Smoothies Out

If you can't bring your own smoothies on the road, you can often purchase them at shops and restaurants. Before you do, though, ask yourself a few simple questions. First, check an ingredient list (you can do this online before you go) and make sure there is no added sugar. Second, check if there is real fruit in the smoothie, rather than fruit flavoring.

Invasion of the Banana Snatchers

The potassium and vitamin C in this icy smoothie are healthier for your kids than snow cones filled with artificial dyes and sugar. Give your kids this refreshing boost instead.

FOUR 1-CUP SERVINGS

1 cup watercress
1 grapefruit, peeled
2 oranges, peeled
1 banana, peeled
1 cup water
2 cups ice

1 Combine all ingredients except ice in a blender, and blend until smooth.

2 Add the ice, and blend until smoothie is slushy and icy.

CALORIES	FAT	PROTEIN	SODIUM	CARBOHYDRATES	SUGARS	FIBER
78	0 grams	2 grams	4 milligrams	20 grams	14 grams	3 grams

MAKE IT FUN: Orange Cubes

Add some decorative fun to your next smoothie or juice with these orange ice cubes. Slice an orange through the middle to create round orange slices. Place each orange slice in the bottom of a muffin tin. Fill the muffin tin with water, covering the orange slice. Freeze until all water is frozen. Pop the orange-sliced frozen ice cubes out and drop into your favorite drinks!

Sweet and Sassy
Strawberry Delight

Grabbing a smoothie on the go doesn't have to be all about the energy and nutrients it can give you. This smoothie still has those things, but above all, it's sweet and delicious.

FOUR 1-CUP SERVINGS

2 oranges, peeled
1 cup strawberries
1 cup blueberries
1 tablespoon flax meal
1 cup coconut milk

1 Place oranges, strawberries, blueberries, flax meal, and ½ cup coconut milk in a blender, and blend at high speed until smooth.

2 Add remaining ½ cup coconut milk, and blend until smoothie is the desired consistency.

CALORIES	FAT	PROTEIN	SODIUM	CARBOHYDRATES	SUGARS	FIBER
113	4 grams	2 grams	11 milligrams	18 grams	12 grams	4 grams

GREEN TIP: Edible Gardening

You can grow beautiful plants in front of your house, and they can be functional and edible as well. Edible plants that produce vibrant-colored flowers and year-round green foliage can replace plants that are decorative only. Try planting asparagus ferns, sunflowers, chives, artichokes, rose hips, the American groundnut, figs, chard, nasturtium flowers, elderberries, passionflowers, rhubarb, or pansies. All these are not only beautiful but edible, too. Add any one of these to smoothies and your yard will serve a greater purpose than just looking nice.

The Cucumber King

Your kids don't need to be particularly fond of cucumbers to love this smoothie. The sweet orange flavor is what they'll notice when they are asking for more.

FOUR 1-CUP SERVINGS

2 cucumbers, peeled
2 oranges, peeled
¼" ginger, peeled
1 cup orange juice
1 cup ice

1 Place cucumbers, oranges, ginger, and ½ cup orange juice in a blender, and blend for 30 seconds on low.

2 Take off lid, and push food onto blades. Add remaining ½ cup juice and ice, and put lid back on. Blend on high until smooth.

CALORIES	FAT	PROTEIN	SODIUM	CARBOHYDRATES	SUGARS	FIBER
85	0 grams	2 grams	4 milligrams	21 grams	14 grams	3 grams

PICKY EATER: Let Kids Choose

Often a picky eater is nothing more than a child trying to exert his or her independence. Give them a little ownership, and watch them make great choices. Rather than choosing between cookies and broccoli, give them choices like strawberries or blueberries. Smoothies are a great way to let kids make good choices. As you get into a routine of smoothie making, kids will begin to learn what things they enjoy in their smoothies. Letting them choose between spinach and romaine lettuce, cucumbers and carrots, or water and orange juice gives them ownership of the drink and lets them be in charge. Once they feel like they were integral in getting this smoothie to the table, they will be less picky, and more likely to drink it.

Parsley Party Punch

Tame your kids' craving for sugary foods by giving them this savory smoothie as you head out for the day. The broccoli and bok choy leaves temper the sweetness from the apples and orange, which is enjoyable to the kids, without it tasting like dessert.

FOUR 1-CUP SERVINGS

1 cup bok choy leaves
2 apples, peeled and
    cored
1 cup broccoli
1 orange, peeled
⅛ cup parsley
2 cups water

1 Place bok choy, apples, broccoli, orange, parsley, and 1 cup water in a blender, and blend for 30 seconds.

2 Add remaining water, and turn blender on again until smoothie is desired consistency.

CALORIES	FAT	PROTEIN	SODIUM	CARBOHYDRATES	SUGARS	FIBER
64	0 grams	1 gram	19 milligrams	16 grams	12 grams	3 grams

TIME SAVER TIP: Freezing Herbs

Ever catch yourself with a pile of herbs and not enough time to use them all before they go bad? Try freezing them. This is perfect for smoothies such as these. Chop your herb, like parsley, into 1-tablespoon portions. Put 1 tablespoon of the herbs into an empty ice cube tray. Fill the ice cube tray with water, covering the herbs. Freeze ice cube tray filled with herbs and water. When frozen, pop out the cubes and store in a freezer-safe bag until you are ready to use them. These herb ice cubes are perfect for smoothies, soups, and sauces.

Help-Me-Hydrate Melon Citrus Juice

This refreshing juice is a thirst quencher! This juice is a healthy and more hydrating alternative to carbonated drinks normally taken to a picnic or to the pool in the summer.

TWO ½-CUP SERVINGS

2 cups watermelon, rind removed

2 oranges, peeled

1 Place watermelon and oranges in a juicer.

2 Run the fruit through the juicer until you have one full cup of juice.

CALORIES	FAT	PROTEIN	SODIUM	CARBOHYDRATES	SUGARS	FIBER
107	0 grams	2 grams	2 milligrams	27 grams	22 grams	4 grams

NUTRITION NEWS: Vitamin C Powerhouse

With both oranges and watermelon in this juice, one serving provides 85 mg of vitamin C. The recommended daily allowance (RDA) for kids ages one to eight years old for vitamin C is 15–25 mg. This drink helps children meet—and exceed—those recommended levels. Vitamin C is essential for those kids who get exposed to germs on a regular basis as it helps protect their immune systems.

Spinapple

Double or triple this recipe because your kids are going to want seconds. Julieanne, one juicing mom, said, "My kids will drink any concoction I make, as long as I put lemon in it!"

ONE 1-CUP SERVING

1 cup baby spinach leaves

1 red apple, peeled and cored

¼ lemon, rind intact

1 celery stalk

1 Juice all ingredients.

2 Mix together until well blended.

CALORIES	FAT	PROTEIN	SODIUM	CARBOHYDRATES	SUGARS	FIBER
172	1 gram	2 grams	56 milligrams	45 grams	34 grams	6 grams

NUTRITION NEWS: Celery for Fluid Balance

The latest dietary recommendations from the USDA suggest increasing our consumption of potassium-containing foods while decreasing sodium intake. Both minerals are necessary for fluid balance. We need our kids to stay hydrated, yet we don't need them retaining water. One cup of celery, with only 19 calories, actually contains 344 mg of potassium and 100 mg of sodium. It is recommended children ages one to eight years old consume 3,000 mg of potassium per day and 1,000 mg of sodium. Mother Nature seems to know just how to package her vegetables for a balance of all the things we need. Any juices that contain celery are perfect for little athletes who need to stay hydrated.

Blazing Blackberries

When kids are away from home for the day, send along this blackberry juice. When it's tough to control what kinds of foods they'll be eating when you aren't around, you can be grateful they are getting some superfoods during the day from this juice.

TWO ⅓-CUP SERVINGS

2 pints blackberries
½ lemon, peeled
1 banana

1 Push blackberries, lemon, and banana through a juicer, and juice completely.

2 Collect into a pitcher, and stir to combine the juices well.

CALORIES	FAT	PROTEIN	SODIUM	CARBOHYDRATES	SUGARS	FIBER
180	2 grams	5 grams	4 milligrams	42 grams	22 grams	17 grams

DIY: Fruit Leather

The ingredients in this juice recipe are perfect for delicious homemade fruit leather. First, use the fruit to make your juice. Second, use the exact same amounts of fruit, and add into a saucepan over medium heat. Stir the fruit until it begins to break down. Add a small amount of your juice, to dilute the fruit in your saucepan. Take the fruit and juice mix, and purée it in a blender or food processor. Line a baking sheet with plastic wrap and pour your fruit onto the wrap. Let the pan dry in the sun, or place in oven at 140°F (or the lowest oven setting) for several hours until the fruit is no longer sticky to the touch. Peel the fruit leather from plastic wrap and eat it!

Aunt Annie's Apple Juice

Next time your family heads out for a hike in the mountains, fill empty water bottles with this apple-grape juice. Partially freeze it to save for the middle of the hike when kids are extra hot and thirsty. It will be refreshing and give them the boost they need to finish the hike!

TWO ½-CUP SERVINGS

2 red Gala apples, cored

1 cup green seedless grapes

1 Push the apples and the grapes through the input spout of a juicer, and juice.

2 Collect the juice in a single container or bottle, and stir to combined both juices.

CALORIES	FAT	PROTEIN	SODIUM	CARBOHYDRATES	SUGARS	FIBER
129	0 grams	1 gram	2 milligrams	34 grams	28 grams	3 grams

MAKE IT FUN: Fizzy Juice

Get a little fizz going in this juice by adding a touch of baking soda to your grape-apple juice. Combine 1 cup juice, ½ cup water, and ½ teaspoon baking soda in a cup. Watch it fizzle. Make sure the baking soda is dissolved before drinking so the juice is smooth, rather than gritty.

Orange C-Shell

Oranges, grapefruits, and lemons are all great sources of vitamin C. The orange brings a delicious sweetness to counteract the tartness of grapefruits and lemons.

THREE ½-CUP SERVINGS

2 oranges, peeled
½ pink grapefruit, peeled
½ lemon, peeled

1 Take oranges, grapefruit, and lemon, and put through the spout of a juicer, one at a time.

2 Collect the juice in a container, and stir before drinking.

CALORIES	FAT	PROTEIN	SODIUM	CARBOHYDRATES	SUGARS	FIBER
57	0 grams	2 grams	0 milligrams	15 grams	11 grams	3 grams

GREEN TIP: Plant a Tree

Teach your kids oranges, grapefruits, and lemons are all grown on a tree. Trees are vital to our environment, and planting a family tree is a great way to contribute. Learn what types of trees are native to your community. Head to a nursery and choose a family tree with fruit that everyone likes. Plant your tree in a special place in your yard. Each year, take a family picture in front of the tree so you can watch the progress and growth. Soon you'll be picking fruits to use in your juices and smoothies!

Smart-N-Tart Lemonade

As a sugar-free sports drink, this sour juice may be just what some child athletes need to get hydrated. One ounce of lemon juice contains six times more potassium than 1 ounce of a lemon-flavored sports drink without the artificial colors and sweeteners.

TWO ½-CUP SERVINGS

2 cucumbers, peeled
1 lemon, peeled

1 Push the cucumbers and lemon through a juicer, and juice until all food has gone through.

2 Collect juice in one glass, and stir to combine.

CALORIES	FAT	PROTEIN	SODIUM	CARBOHYDRATES	SUGARS	FIBER
53	0 grams	2 grams	6 milligrams	14 grams	6 grams	2 grams

TIME SAVER TIP: Juicing Lemons

Juicing lemons and limes without a juicer is not only possible but quite simple. There are a few tricks to extracting the most juice out of these citrus fruits. Trick number one, warm up a lemon or lime in the microwave for about 20–30 seconds. The juice of a warm fruit will flow much more freely than a cold one. Second, roll the fruit around on the counter with the palm of your hand. This will break up some of the membranes of the fruit. Then, the fruit is ready to cut and squeeze. More juice is extracted this way than you can get squeezing juice from a cold, unsoftened fruit.

Garden Goose Juice

Forget about spending the next day trying to use up your zucchini for bread. Spend 5 minutes and juice it instead. Adding some apples to this zucchini juice brings out the sweetness of the fall flavors.

TWO ½-CUP SERVINGS

1 green zucchini
3 carrots, peeled
2 red apples, cored

1 Juice the zucchini, carrots, and apples into one large glass.

2 Stir the juices together until they are thoroughly combined.

CALORIES	FAT	PROTEIN	SODIUM	CARBOHYDRATES	SUGARS	FIBER
138	1 gram	3 grams	82 milligrams	34 grams	24 grams	6 grams

GREEN TIP: Repurpose Pulp

Depending on the condition of your pulp after running fruits and vegetables through the juicer, there may be something you can do with it. If your pulp is very dry, the best thing to do with it may be to turn it onto a compost pile, or bury it in your garden to promote soil turnover. However, if your pulp still has a little water to it, you can use it in baked goods, such as muffins. Be sure to use organic fruits and vegetables, or wash your fruits and vegetables thoroughly if you are using the pulp. Using pulp from this recipe, with the carrots, zucchini, and apples, would make a delicious addition to zucchini bread or carrot cake.

Sippin' Celery Soda

*When the kids are asking for apple juice, don't be afraid to add
a little celery to their cup. As an excellent source of vitamins C and K,
celery boosts the nutritional value of plain apple juice.*

THREE ½-CUP SERVINGS

1 Granny Smith apple,
   cored
2 celery stalks

1 Juice the apple and then the celery.

2 Collect in a single container, and stir before
    serving.

CALORIES	FAT	PROTEIN	SODIUM	CARBOHYDRATES	SUGARS	FIBER
30	0 grams	0 grams	21 milligrams	7 grams	6 grams	1 gram

NUTRITION NEWS: Potassium

Blood pressure, muscle growth, brain function, and the nervous system are all
affected by potassium. Besides celery, other potassium sources include raisins, prunes, apricots, dates, strawberries, and melons. It's important to note
that young athletes may need more potassium than other kids. Potassium and
sodium help maintain fluid balance even while sweating. A good goal for potassium intake is 4,700 mg per day.

Double Yum Plum

*Don't just survive the next car ride with your kids, enjoy it.
Kids with low blood sugar strapped into their car seats are
a recipe for disaster. Hand them this drink. It will lift blood
sugar to a level that will put smiles on their faces.*

TWO ½-CUP SERVINGS

1½ cups cherries,
    pitted
2 black plums, pitted

1 Push cherries and plums through the spout of a juicer, and turn on.

2 Continue to push the fruit through until it has all been juiced.

3 Collect the juice in a single container, and stir before serving.

CALORIES	FAT	PROTEIN	SODIUM	CARBOHYDRATES	SUGARS	FIBER
55	0 grams	1 gram	0 milligrams	14 grams	11 grams	2 grams

GREEN TIP: Road Trips

While driving to your next vacation may feel like an eco-fail, there are things you can do on your road trip to save resources. An exciting thing to do on family vacations is to stop at roadside farm stands and buy local produce. Visiting Oregon? Try their amazing blueberries. Visiting Georgia? Grab some peaches along the road. Visiting California? Don't forget to pick up lemons and oranges. Get out of the car, talk to the farmers, and enjoy fresh fruits and vegetables right in the very place they were grown.

Icy Island Dream

No need to head to the tropics to have a taste of the islands at home. A ripe papaya, a juicy pineapple, and some bright red strawberries can take you and your kids on a mini vacation even in the middle of winter.

THREE ½-CUP SERVINGS

1 cup pineapple, peeled
7 large strawberries, hull intact
½ papaya, seeds removed

1 Take pineapple, strawberries, and papaya, place in a juicer, one after the other, and juice.

2 Collect juice from all three fruits into one container, and stir before serving to combine.

CALORIES	FAT	PROTEIN	SODIUM	CARBOHYDRATES	SUGARS	FIBER
56	0 grams	1 gram	2 milligrams	14 grams	10 grams	2 grams

MAKE IT FUN: Strawberry Delights!

When you purchase a pound of strawberries, save seven strawberries for this juice, and use the rest to have some fun. Instead of frosting sugar-filled cookies, let kids decorate nutrient-filled strawberries. Using toothpicks and clean dry strawberries, dip in melted chocolate. Before the chocolate sets, dip a second time in sprinkles, nuts, shredded coconut, or sugar crystals. Let dry completely on wax paper and enjoy.

Power Peach Punch

*Pick up a whole box of peaches so you'll have enough fruit
to eat some fresh as well as to make this delicious peach
strawberry juice. The kids will enjoy the fruity taste.*

THREE ½-CUP SERVINGS

1 large peach, pitted

**7 large strawberries,
hulls intact**

1 Take peach and strawberries, push through the
spout of a juicer, and juice.

2 Collect juice into a single container, and stir
till juices are well blended.

CALORIES	FAT	PROTEIN	SODIUM	CARBOHYDRATES	SUGARS	FIBER
28	0 grams	1 gram	0 milligrams	7 grams	5 grams	1 gram

TIME SAVER TIP: Delegate Tasks

You are trying to get out the door, but there is too much to do. Have your kids
lend a hand. Have one child prep the fruit, one child run the juicer, and one
child clean up the mess. Have them trade off so no one gets stuck on cleanup
duty all the time.

Summer Lemon Splash

This lemon-cucumber water is perfect for taking to the swimming pool during the hot days of summer. It's refreshing and light, and great for hydrating on the go.

FOUR ½-CUP SERVINGS

1 lemon, peeled
2 cucumbers, peeled
1 cup ice cold water

1 Juice lemon and cucumber.

2 Stir in ice cold water until it is all combined.

CALORIES	FAT	PROTEIN	SODIUM	CARBOHYDRATES	SUGARS	FIBER
26	0 grams	1 gram	3 milligrams	7 grams	3 grams	1 gram

DIY: Get the Most Out of Your Lemons

One normal-size lemon should yield about 4 tablespoons of juice. Keep extra lemon juice in the fridge for a quick drop into plain water, for flavoring up main dishes like chicken or fish, or to add to sauces.

Sugar Plum Fairy Juice

Vitamin C does more than strengthen immunity, it can also help us absorb iron better. This plum and pineapple juice is packed with the iron-absorbing vitamin C your kids need for more energy.

THREE ½-CUP SERVINGS

2 black plums, pit removed

1 cup pineapple, rind removed

1 Juice the plums and pineapple into a single container.

2 Stir and pour into individual cups.

CALORIES	FAT	PROTEIN	SODIUM	CARBOHYDRATES	SUGARS	FIBER
47	0 grams	1 gram	1 milligram	12 grams	10 grams	1 gram

NUTRITION NEWS: Magnesium

Plums and pineapples are both great sources of magnesium, necessary for proper bone development. It's an essential nutrient, meaning that our bodies cannot produce it on their own. We need to eat foods rich in magnesium every single day. Magnesium, calcium, and phosphorus all work together to build bone and muscle tissue. While plums and pineapples are good sources of magnesium, so are Swiss chard, spinach, and pumpkin seeds.

Cucumbers and Crocodile Juice

The strong flavors in pineapple juice make it a perfect fruit to pair with any vegetable. The cucumbers add a fresh and subtle flair to this citrus drink that kids will enjoy. Cucumbers don't always need a dip for kids to eat them.

TWO ½-CUP SERVINGS

1 cucumber, peeled
1 cup pineapple, peeled

1 Juice the cucumber and the pineapple one at a time.

2 Collect in a single container, and stir before serving.

CALORIES	FAT	PROTEIN	SODIUM	CARBOHYDRATES	SUGARS	FIBER
63	0 grams	1 gram	4 milligrams	16 grams	11 grams	2 grams

PICKY EATER: Cucumber Water

Make some refreshing cucumber water without serving cucumber in the water. Fill a pitcher of water. Drop in chunks of chopped up cucumbers into the water, and put in the fridge overnight. In the morning, remove the cucumber, or strain through a sieve so you are left with the cucumber-flavored water. This drink is a refreshing summer substitute for lemonade when served over a cup full of ice and garnished with slices of lemon.

Super Supreme Tangerine

Citrus drinks don't always need to be orange juice or lemonade. This combination of pineapple and tangerine will give kids the benefits of the vitamin C with the less run-of-the-mill flavors of tropical fruits.

TWO ⅓-CUP SERVINGS

1 cup pineapple, peeled

1 tangerine, peeled

1 Juice the pineapple and the tangerine, and collect into a single cup.

2 Stir to combine juices, and pour into two different cups to serve.

CALORIES	FAT	PROTEIN	SODIUM	CARBOHYDRATES	SUGARS	FIBER
70	0 grams	1 gram	2 milligrams	18 grams	14 grams	2 grams

DIY: Peeling Tangerines

Tangerines are a simple fruit for kids to peel. Even the very youngest child will have fun peeling tangerines. Consider a contest to make it more fun. The child who can peel the tangerine, getting the peel to come off of the fruit in one continuous piece, wins. This ongoing contest is a fun challenge for kids. The more often they practice, the better they will get at it. When this fruit can be peeled with one peel, it's fun to trick other people by putting it together, with no fruit inside.

A Pair of Pears

Bring this pear-and-apple juice on your evening walks. Children will love the variety of adding a dash of pear and lemon to an old favorite.

TWO ½-CUP SERVINGS

2 Bartlett pears
2 Red Delicious apples
¼ lemon, peeled

1 Juice the pears, apples, and lemon into a single cup or pitcher.

2 Mix the three juices thoroughly. Strain through a coffee filter for thinner consistency, if desired.

CALORIES	FAT	PROTEIN	SODIUM	CARBOHYDRATES	SUGARS	FIBER
114	0 grams	1 gram	0 milligrams	30 grams	22 grams	5 grams

PICKY EATER: Trail Mix

Kids who don't like the soft, often mushy, texture of fresh pears may like dried pears chopped up into trail mix. Let the kids make their own trail mix by having bowls of different ingredients, and let them put together their own baggie. First, include bowls of chopped dried pears, dried apricots, raisins, dried cranberries, or dried apples. Second, have bowls full of nuts like pecans, walnuts, almonds, cashews, and peanuts. Third, include a small treat like mini chocolate chips or mini chocolate-covered candies like M&M's. Let them bring the trail mix with you on your next hike or outing.

Partridge in a Pear Tree

*"Pear"fect for optimal digestion, pineapples and pears
are gentle on little tummies.*

FOUR ½-CUP SERVINGS

½ pineapple, skin and
   core removed
2 Bartlett pears, cored
1 lemon, peeled

1 Juice the pineapple, pears, and lemon into a
single pitcher or cup.

2 Mix thoroughly in order for all juices to be well
combined.

CALORIES	FAT	PROTEIN	SODIUM	CARBOHYDRATES	SUGARS	FIBER
78	0 grams	1 gram	1 milligram	21 grams	14 grams	4 grams

TIME SAVER TIP: Storing Juices

Make juice today, and then drink it tomorrow. The ultimate time saver is to be able to do things ahead of time and have them ready. While homemade juice tastes best when it's fresh, it's not always convenient for families with small children to drink it right away. Juice from melons does not store well and should be consumed right away. Store other juices in the fridge, in an airtight and opaque container. Drink within 3 days. Shake or stir again prior to drinking, as stored juices will separate. If you plan to store it longer, freeze the juice until you are ready to drink. Some fruits, like grapes, can also be stored as juice through proper canning methods.

Pelican Pickle Juice

Pickle juice to drink? You bet! This juice includes the crisp flavors of a cucumber with the sweetness of dill—but not the vinegar taste. Kids will enjoy this palatable juice.

THREE ½-CUP SERVINGS

½ large cucumber, peeled
1 celery stalk, leaves intact
2 sprigs fresh baby dill

1 Juice the cucumber and celery into a single container.

2 Stir well and garnish with dill. Allow the flavors to blend in the refrigerator.

CALORIES	FAT	PROTEIN	SODIUM	CARBOHYDRATES	SUGARS	FIBER
10	0 grams	0 grams	12 milligrams	2 grams	1 gram	0 grams

GREEN TIP: Growing Contest

Whether your kids plant vegetables like cucumbers, or herbs like dill, encourage a friendly contest to make it exciting. State fairs all over the country have competitions relating to how big, how beautiful, and how tasty kids (or adults) can grow their produce. Have your own fair after the harvest and judge each child's produce in different categories. Even offer a blue ribbon for each category. A second judging can happen after the kids make something with their vegetables or herbs. The best juice or smoothie can be entered in your mini family fair contest.

4

Better Snacks for Better Kids:

DRINKS WITH A PURPOSE

Using smoothies or juices to heal our children, help them grow, or build their immunity is not only smart, it's essential. Food can truly be their medicine if we use it right. It isn't necessary for all kids to have ear infections, or to get the flu every winter. The stronger our kids' immune systems, the better prepared they will be to fight off infections without us ever knowing they have been exposed.

Fruits and vegetables that are high in vitamins, minerals, and antioxidants have the building blocks necessary for our kids' bodies to function at an optimal level. Kids who are fed nutrient-depleted foods, such as potato chips and candy, that are full of disease-promoting fats and sugars, won't stand a chance at staying well when germs are shared on the playground. Even a multivitamin won't give them the protection they need. All the components of fruits and vegetables work together to help kids absorb the nutrients they specifically need, in the amounts their bodies need.

Use this section of smoothies and juices to help your kids stay healthy and also give them the necessary nutrients to grow strong bones, have better memory, improve digestion, have great skin, and prevent future chronic disease, aches, and pains.

Ginger and Spice and Everything Nice

MOTION SICKNESS: Take this smoothie on your next road trip. Prepare the night before and store in the fridge in a cup with a lid. Take out of the fridge as you head out the door and give it a good shake.

FOUR 1-CUP SERVINGS

1" ginger, peeled and sliced
¾ cup almond milk
1 teaspoon ground cloves
1 cup baby greens (or baby spinach)
1 banana, peeled

1 Place ginger, almond milk, cloves, greens, and banana in a high-powered blender.

2 Blend long enough that all the fruit, greens, and spices are well blended.

CALORIES	FAT	PROTEIN	SODIUM	CARBOHYDRATES	SUGARS	FIBER
60	1 gram	2 grams	32 milligrams	11 grams	6 grams	2 grams

NUTRITION NEWS: Let Ginger Be Your Medicine

From birth, my children have always gotten sick in the car. After many road trips that ended in an upset stomach disaster, we began to medicate with ginger. Perfect for a road trip, the ginger in this smoothie has been shown in double-blind placebo studies to prevent motion sickness, nausea, and dizziness. Ginger is a safe and natural alternative to antinausea drugs for kids.

A Sweet Beet Treat

HEART HEALTH: Whether it's Valentine's Day or your kids just love the color pink, this pink smoothie will make them smile.

FOUR 1-CUP SERVINGS

1 cup beet greens

3 beets, peeled and chopped

1 banana, peeled

1 cup almond milk

½ cup ice cubes

1 Place beet greens, chopped beets, banana, and ½ cup almond milk in a blender.

2 Blend until smooth.

3 Add the remainder of the almond milk and the ice cubes, and blend until creamy.

CALORIES	FAT	PROTEIN	SODIUM	CARBOHYDRATES	SUGARS	FIBER
87	1 gram	4 grams	85 milligrams	16 grams	10 grams	3 grams

GREEN TIP: No Waste Greens!

Beets are known for their rich color and high amount of antioxidants. However, many people keep the root and throw out the greens! These beet greens are a nutrient powerhouse, and there is no reason to have them go to waste. The vitamin K alone in 1 cup of beet greens has eight times more vitamin K than kids usually get in a day.

Wacky Watermelon

DIGESTION: When watermelon gets to 10 cents per pound in the summer, it's a good idea to stock up! The problem, however, is once it's cut, it doesn't last long. Add it to this smoothie once you've had enough slices, and it won't go to waste.

FOUR 1-CUP SERVINGS

1 cup radicchio leaves
1 tablespoon flax meal
½ sprig mint leaves
2 cups watermelon
1 cucumber, peeled
¼ cup water

1 Put all ingredients in a blender.

2 Mix until smooth.

CALORIES	FAT	PROTEIN	SODIUM	CARBOHYDRATES	SUGARS	FIBER
42	1 gram	1 gram	2 milligrams	9 grams	6 grams	1 gram

GREEN TIP: Grow Your Own Mint

Kids who grow their own foods are more likely to eat the foods they grow. Mint is an easy herb to grow and perfect for beginning gardeners. A simple flower pot for the windowsill, soil, and mint seeds are all you need to start a garden. Once your plant has a few leaves, simply pinch off a leaf and use it in your smoothies. As long as a third of the plant is still attached, it will continue to grow.

Prince Papaya Potion

IMMUNITY: No need to slave over chicken noodle soup on the days your kids are sick or under the weather. Fill them up with this immunity-boosting papaya smoothie instead and they'll be on the road to recovery in no time.

FOUR 1-CUP SERVINGS

1 cup romaine lettuce

2 papayas, seeds removed

1 cup strawberries

1 cup water

1 Place romaine lettuce, papayas, and strawberries in a blender. Pour in ½ cup water, and blend until smooth.

2 Continue to blend as you pour in the remaining ½ cup water until it is the consistency you prefer.

CALORIES	FAT	PROTEIN	SODIUM	CARBOHYDRATES	SUGARS	FIBER
73	0 grams	1 gram	6 milligrams	18 grams	11 grams	4 grams

NUTRITION NEWS: Papaya

Papaya's superfood status comes from its ability to aid in digestion, reduce inflammation, and protect against cell damage. Papayas are a good source of folate, potassium, and vitamins A, C, E, and K. The enzymes present in papayas assist with digestion of proteins and are so effective that they are packaged and sold as supplements. The vitamins available in papaya work together with the enzymes to reduce inflammation; for that reason, asthma and arthritis sufferers can find relief by eating papaya. One study showed damaged skin from burns healed faster when taking these vitamins together, as found in papayas.

Green Goji Giant

IMMUNITY: If you are finding it hard to get your hands on some goji berries, try growing them yourself. As with other berries, the properties provided by the vitamins will help your kids stay healthy this winter and strengthen their immune systems.

FOUR 1-CUP SERVINGS

1 cup spinach
2 bananas, peeled
2 cups goji berries
1 cup Greek-style yogurt

1 Combine spinach, bananas, berries, and ½ cup yogurt in a blender, and blend for 20 seconds.

2 Add remaining yogurt, and blend for 30 seconds to 1 minute, or until all food is processed and smooth.

CALORIES	FAT	PROTEIN	SODIUM	CARBOHYDRATES	SUGARS	FIBER
130	0 grams	7 grams	31 milligrams	27 grams	17 grams	3 grams

DIY: Make Greek-Style Yogurt

Because Greek-style yogurt is concentrated, you get more protein and health benefits from eating it as compared to regular yogurt. It's simple to make if you don't want to spend the extra money on commercially prepared Greek-style yogurt. Use homemade yogurt or plain yogurt from the store. Scoop out the plain yogurt into a sheet of cheesecloth or a very fine strainer. Place over a bowl to catch the liquid drippings. Place in fridge. After yogurt is reduced to half, about 24 hours later, scoop the thick yogurt that remains on top of your strainer for your high-protein Greek-style yogurt. Store in the fridge for 5–7 days.

Cranberry Cosmic Cup

IMMUNITY: Cranberries and blueberries are just what the doctor ordered for kids suffering from bladder infections. Don't wait for the infection to present itself, however. Protect kids with this smoothie before they get sick.

FOUR 1-CUP SERVINGS

1 cup romaine lettuce
2 cups blueberries
1 cup cranberries
1 apple, cored and peeled
1 banana, peeled
½" ginger, peeled
2 cups water

1 Take romaine lettuce, blueberries, cranberries, apple, banana, ginger, and 1 cup water, and put in blender. Blend until it is smooth.

2 Continue to blend, and slowly pour in the last cup of water until mixture reaches the desired consistency.

CALORIES	FAT	PROTEIN	SODIUM	CARBOHYDRATES	SUGARS	FIBER
130	1 gram	2 grams	9 milligrams	30 grams	16 grams	6 grams

NUTRITION NEWS: Cranberries

The antioxidant responsible for cranberry's ability to prevent and treat urinary tract infection is called proanthocyanidin. With high amounts of this antioxidant in cranberries, this little fruit is super effective at healing. Proanthocyanidins have the ability to prevent and block infection, causing bacteria like *E. coli* from attaching to the lining of the urinary tract. Cranberries also have the ability to acidify urine, helping to prevent against kidney stones. So don't wait to eat cranberries at Thanksgiving. Make sure your kids are getting some all year.

Peace, Love, and Pineapple Smoothie

ANTI-INFLAMMATION: Escape to the tropics with this pineapple-and-orange medley of flavors. Pineapple's high amount of manganese is perfect to give athletes energy while at the same time reducing inflammation due to injury.

FOUR 1-CUP SERVINGS

1 cup spinach
2 cups pineapple, peeled and cored
1 orange, peeled
2 apples, peeled and cored
1 tablespoon flax meal
2 cups orange juice

1 Take spinach, pineapple, orange, apples, flax meal, and 1 cup orange juice, and place in a high-powered blender. Blend until smooth.

2 Add the remaining orange juice, and continue to blend until it reaches desired consistency.

CALORIES	FAT	PROTEIN	SODIUM	CARBOHYDRATES	SUGARS	FIBER
158	0 grams	2 grams	9 milligrams	40 grams	30 grams	4 grams

TIME SAVER TIP: Finding Recipes

Have a system for flagging recipes your kids particularly like so you can quickly go back to them without scouring all your cookbooks to find them again. If your kids love this pineapple smoothie, and you noticed they drank it without complaint, use the Post-it Page Markers or Half-inch Flags to mark the page. Color coordinate according to which child liked it. Susie's favorite recipes could all be flagged with a red Post-it tab, while Johnny's could be all green.

Choo-Choo Chuggin' Cherry

ANTI-INFLAMMATION: The anti-inflammatory properties in cherries make this smoothie perfect for active kids. Prepare this drink for afternoon refreshment, after a long day of playing outside. Freeze extra cherries to float on top of the drink.

FOUR 1-CUP SERVINGS

1 cup spinach

2 cups cherries, pitted

1 apple, cored and peeled

Pulp of 1 vanilla bean, or 1 teaspoon vanilla extract

2 cups water

1 Combine spinach, cherries, apple, vanilla bean, and 1 cup water in a blender. Blend until smooth.

2 Add remaining 1 cup water, and blend again until all ingredients are well incorporated.

CALORIES	FAT	PROTEIN	SODIUM	CARBOHYDRATES	SUGARS	FIBER
70	0 grams	1 gram	6 milligrams	18 grams	14 grams	2 grams

NUTRITION NEWS: Cherries

A 2010 study published in the *Journal of the International Society of Sport Nutrition* found tart cherry juice reduced pain during long-distance running. The antioxidants in the cherries seemed to protect against damage caused by trauma to the muscles. The benefit of the cherry juice was seen in both participants in the study who drank the juice prior to an endurance event as well as during the event. Cherry juice's anti-inflammatory properties can benefit regular athletes as well as endurance athletes.

Kool Kollosal Kale

IMMUNITY: Get an immune boost with this kale-and-carrot combination. Bugs this winter won't stand a chance in your home, and your kids will have to go to school every day, much to their chagrin.

TWO 1-CUP SERVINGS

2 kale leaves

4 carrots, peeled and chopped

1 apple, cored and peeled

1 banana, peeled

2 cups water

1 Place kale, carrots, apple, and banana in blender.

2 Pour water in slowly, and blend until the smoothie reaches the desired consistency.

CALORIES	FAT	PROTEIN	SODIUM	CARBOHYDRATES	SUGARS	FIBER
164	1 gram	3 grams	111 milligrams	40 grams	22 grams	7 grams

NUTRITION NEWS: Kale

The combination of vitamins and minerals in kale makes it a great vegetable to strengthen kids' immunity. Vitamin C has been shown to prevent recurring ear infections and strengthen kids against the common cold. Kale has the most vitamin C of all the leafy greens at almost 200 percent of the recommended daily allowance in 1 cup. With an excellent rating for more than 10 other vitamins and minerals, kale truly is a superfood!

Pomegranate Power Punch

HYDRATION: Pomegranates' super supply of antioxidants makes this smoothie a great recovery drink for active young kids. Antioxidants accelerate healing of damaged muscle tissue from tough workouts. The potassium from the banana and orange juice helps kids stay adequately hydrated and ready for the next adventure.

FOUR 1-CUP SERVINGS

1 cup iceberg lettuce
2 cups pomegranate pips
1 orange, peeled
1 banana, peeled
1 cup pomegranate juice

1 Place all ingredients in high-powered blender to blend.

2 Continue to blend until consistency is smooth.

CALORIES	FAT	PROTEIN	SODIUM	CARBOHYDRATES	SUGARS	FIBER
149	1 gram	3 grams	10 milligrams	35 grams	17 grams	5 grams

DIY: Opening a Pomegranate

Opening a pomegranate doesn't need to be messy or stain your clothes. First, choose a pomegranate that is heavy for its size. Cut the top off of the pomegranate, approximately 1" from the root. Cut shallow slices through the skin around the fruit. Submerge entire fruit in water, and peel the skin back at the points the skin has been scored. Push the seeds out with your finger and into the bowl of water. The seeds will sink to the bottom. You can remove the skin from the water and drain the seeds through a strainer.

Blackberry Bonanza

STRONG BONES: Growing kids need calcium and magnesium for bone growth and development. This smoothie contains both and is critical during those growth spurts.

FOUR 1-CUP SERVINGS

1 cup romaine lettuce
1 pint blackberries
1 cup pineapple, peeled and cored
2 bananas, peeled
1 cup Greek-style yogurt

1 Place lettuce, blackberries, pineapple, bananas, and ½ cup yogurt in a blender, and blend until smooth.

2 Add the remaining ½ cup yogurt, and blend again until desired consistency is achieved.

CALORIES	FAT	PROTEIN	SODIUM	CARBOHYDRATES	SUGARS	FIBER
139	1 gram	8 grams	26 milligrams	29 grams	17 grams	6 grams

NUTRITION NEWS: Synergy of Nutrients

Most likely you've heard that calcium is essential to strong bones. However, calcium is only effective in the presence of other vitamins and minerals, such as vitamin D and magnesium. Other vitamins that effect bone health are A, B_{12}, C, and K. The nutrients from other foods in this smoothie, like the calcium from the yogurt and the magnesium in the blackberries, provide the building blocks necessary to build better bones, more than a calcium supplement alone could do. Have your kids drink this smoothie in the sun to get a dose of vitamin D, and they'll be set for great bone health.

Fresh Flaxle Rock

DIGESTION: Adding flaxseed to smoothies is a great way to keep your kids regular. Combine the soluble fiber in the flax with the insoluble fiber of the orange in this drink, and it's a recipe for perfect digestion.

FOUR 1-CUP SERVINGS

½ cup cantaloupe
1 banana, peeled
1 orange, peeled
1 cup raspberries
1 tablespoon flaxseed
2 cups water

1 Combine cantaloupe, banana, orange, raspberries, flaxseed, and 1 cup water in a blender, and blend.

2 Continue to blend, and add remaining water until smoothie is smooth.

CALORIES	FAT	PROTEIN	SODIUM	CARBOHYDRATES	SUGARS	FIBER
72	1 gram	2 grams	4 milligrams	16 grams	10 grams	4 grams

NUTRITION NEWS: Flaxseed

Flaxseed is a great source of omega-3s, fiber, lignan (a type of phytoestrogen that acts like an antioxidant and is linked to lower cancer rates), and B vitamins. Flaxseed has been shown in research to reduce cancer risk, control blood pressure, protect bones, and promote brain development. It can be added to many foods, such as smoothies, without changing the taste or texture.

Pineapple Pix-C

MENTAL HEALTH: A study published in Neuroscience *showed vitamin C has a calming effect on children. This smoothie is loaded with vitamin C if you are interested in well-behaved and healthy kids.*

FOUR 1-CUP SERVINGS

1 cup watercress
2 oranges, peeled
½ pineapple, peeled and cored
½ lemon, peeled
½ lime, peeled
1 cup pineapple juice

1 Place watercress, oranges, pineapple, lemon, lime, and ½ cup juice in a blender, and blend.

2 Continue to blend while pouring in remaining ½ cup juice. Keep blending until texture is smooth and fruit is incorporated.

CALORIES	FAT	PROTEIN	SODIUM	CARBOHYDRATES	SUGARS	FIBER
126	0 grams	2 grams	6 milligrams	32 grams	24 grams	4 grams

TIME SAVER TIP: Canned Pineapple

Fresh pineapple tastes great and is high in vitamins and minerals. However, fresh pineapple isn't always that easy to find and prepare—and it isn't always affordable. During the off season, canned pineapple can be substituted for fresh. When choosing canned pineapple, choose 100-percent juice or "in its own juice" to avoid added sugars and syrups. After using the pineapple flesh for your smoothie, use the juice for the liquid, or pour the pineapple juice into an ice pop mold for an after-dinner treat.

Astro-Nuts

*BRAIN SUPPORT: Astronauts have to be smart! Smoothies like
this one with flaxseed and almonds are high in omega-3s,
shown to support and promote healthy brain development.*

FOUR 1-CUP SERVINGS

2 cups almond milk
¼ cup almonds
1 tablespoon flaxseed
1 cup spinach
2 cups strawberries
3 rhubarb stalks

1 Combine 1 cup almond milk with almonds and flaxseed in a blender. Blend completely until smooth and creamy.

2 Add spinach, strawberries, and rhubarb, and blend again until smooth.

3 Add remaining 1 cup almond milk, and blend until desired consistency of smoothie is reached.

CALORIES	FAT	PROTEIN	SODIUM	CARBOHYDRATES	SUGARS	FIBER
141	6 grams	7 grams	70 milligrams	17 grams	9 grams	4 grams

NUTRITION NEWS: Omega-3s

Kids need omega-3s. A deficiency in omega-3s can present itself as depression, fatigue, joint pain, and dry itchy skin. Including omega-3s in your kids' diet will not only help alleviate some of these symptoms but can also reduce inflammation, promote healthy cell membranes, and support brain development. Just 2 tablespoons of flaxseed has more omega-3s than any other food source shown to be a good source of omega-3s. These other sources include salmon, walnuts, sardines, shrimp, and tuna.

Rocking Lemon-Melon

HYDRATION: This smoothie delivers ultimate hydration for kids on those hot summer days. It's hard sometimes to come in from the heat and fun just to drink a glass of water, but delivering this cool, refreshing smoothie to them during play is a hydrating treat they'll take a break for.

FOUR 1-CUP SERVINGS

1 cup romaine lettuce
2 cups seedless
    watermelon
2 cups cantaloupe
½ lemon, peeled
½ lime, peeled
2 cups water

1 Combine romaine, watermelon, cantaloupe, lemon, lime, and 1 cup water in a blender, and blend about 30 seconds.

2 Add remaining 1 cup water, and blend until smoothie is desired consistency.

CALORIES	FAT	PROTEIN	SODIUM	CARBOHYDRATES	SUGARS	FIBER
53	0 grams	1 gram	14 milligrams	13 grams	11 grams	1 gram

MAKE IT FUN: The Watermelon Bowl

Don't toss the watermelon rind after making this smoothie. Cut the watermelon in half across the middle to scoop out the flesh for the smoothie. Keep the watermelon rind intact. Use a melon baller to scoop balls of cantaloupe, watermelon, and honeydew melon. Add to your watermelon bowl, then add strawberries, blueberries, and chopped pineapple. Grate ginger over the top, and stir. Your watermelon bowl fruit salad makes a beautiful and fun centerpiece!

Vita-Mint Shake

DIGESTION: Mint has an antispasmodic effect on the muscles in the digestive tract. Indigestion, heartburn, gas, and tummy aches will be alleviated by including mint in this smoothie.

FOUR 1-CUP SERVINGS

2 cups cantaloupe, rind
  and seeds removed
1 cucumber, peeled
2 tablespoons mint
  leaves
¼" ginger, peeled
1 cup distilled water

1 Place cantaloupe, cucumber, mint, ginger, and ½ cup water into a blender, and blend for 30 seconds.

2 Continue to blend while slowly adding the remaining ½ cup water until the smoothie is smooth enough to drink.

CALORIES	FAT	PROTEIN	SODIUM	CARBOHYDRATES	SUGARS	FIBER
37	0 grams	1 gram	14 milligrams	9 grams	7 grams	1 gram

GREEN TIP: Square-Foot Gardening

Living in small quarters doesn't mean you can't have a garden anymore. Beginning and advanced gardeners both can be successful with a small garden. Less water, less seeds, and less space, with just as much yield, are possible with square-foot gardening. You will only need 6" of soil and a 1' × 1' block of space. Plant your seeds and watch your food grow. Start gardening today with some mint seeds, and you'll be able to make this smoothie in as little as 6 weeks.

Green Grassy Goblets

ANTICANCER: Reducing the risk for cancer and heart disease for children starts with increasing their greens. This smoothie is the ultimate "salad in a glass." With four different greens in this smoothie, you can be sure your kids are getting a variety of important nutrients, without adding high-fat salad dressings.

FOUR 1-CUP SERVINGS

1 cup spinach
2 kale leaves
1 cup wheatgrass
1 celery stalk
½ lemon, peeled
2 cups orange juice

1 Combine spinach, kale, wheatgrass, celery, lemon, and 1 cup orange juice in a blender, and blend for 30 seconds.

2 Add remaining 1 cup orange juice, and continue to blend until smooth, about 60–90 seconds.

CALORIES	FAT	PROTEIN	SODIUM	CARBOHYDRATES	SUGARS	FIBER
73	0 grams	2 grams	23 milligrams	17 grams	11 grams	1 gram

DIY: Growing Wheatgrass

Juicing wheatgrass or using it in smoothies can be expensive, unless you sprout your own. Wheat berries can be purchased for very little cost, but you will need to purchase a sprouting tray for proper growing. Once you have a sprouting tray, follow the directions for your specific product. You can have your own wheatgrass within 7–15 days of planting. Continue to harvest and grow new wheatgrass every two weeks for smoothies and juices made to order.

Best Smellin' Melon Smoothie

ANTICANCER: The American Cancer Society recommends eating five different fruits and vegetables per day to reduce cancer risk. With five fruits and vegetables in this smoothie, your kids will be off to a good start.

FOUR 1-CUP SERVINGS

1 cup romaine lettuce

2 cups cantaloupe, rind and seeds removed

2 carrots, peeled

1 cup pineapple, skin removed

1 beet, peeled and chopped

2 cups water

1 Place romaine, cantaloupe, carrots, pineapple, beet, and 1 cup water in a blender, and blend until smooth.

2 Add the remaining 1 cup water, and continue to blend until all fruits and vegetables are well incorporated.

CALORIES	FAT	PROTEIN	SODIUM	CARBOHYDRATES	SUGARS	FIBER
72	0 grams	2 grams	54 milligrams	17 grams	13 grams	3 grams

MAKE IT FUN: Eat a Rainbow

With orange, red, yellow, and green, this smoothie has a variety of colors. For optimal cancer prevention and lifelong health, it's vital our kids eat (or drink!) a rainbow of fruits and vegetables each day. This can actually be a fun thing to track with kids. Outline a rainbow in pen or pencil on some paper and hang it on the fridge. As soon as your child eats a fruit or vegetable, take a crayon of the same color, and color a stripe on your fridge rainbow. Once the rainbow is complete, your child will know he or she ate a variety of colors that day.

Coconut Craziness

IMMUNITY: While vitamin C helps to prevent colds and flu, coconuts may help to fight them. Recent studies suggest that certain fats in coconut, such as lauric acid, can kill bacteria, viruses, and even fungi and yeast.

FOUR 1-CUP SERVINGS

1 cup iceberg lettuce
Flesh of 2 coconuts
1 tablespoon honey
1 cup coconut milk

1 Combine iceberg lettuce, coconut flesh, honey, and coconut milk in a blender.

2 Blend on high until smoothie reaches desired consistency.

CALORIES	FAT	PROTEIN	SODIUM	CARBOHYDRATES	SUGARS	FIBER
46	3 grams	0 grams	9 milligrams	5 grams	5 grams	0 grams

DIY: Cutting a Coconut

Opening a coconut can be intimidating. The tough outer shell is thick, and your usual kitchen knife isn't up to the task. To open a coconut, first, using a hammer, pierce the indentations on the top of the coconut with an ice pick or long nail. Drain the coconut water out of the coconut through the pierced hole into a bowl. Next, using a hammer, gently tap around the equator of the coconut, rotating to hit all sides. The coconut should split in half at this point. Place both halves in the oven at 400°F for about 10 minutes. The coconut flesh is now ready to scoop out.

Mango Madness

ENERGY AND HEART HEALTH: Active kids can benefit from the bananas and mangoes in this smoothie. These fruits provide increased energy from the fruit sugar and good carbohydrates. It also contributes to cardiovascular benefits from the potassium. The smoothie is the perfect combination for active kids.

FOUR 1-CUP SERVINGS

½ cup dandelion greens
½ cup romaine lettuce
2 mangoes, peeled and
    pit removed
1 banana, peeled
½ cup water

1 Place dandelion greens, romaine, mangoes, banana, and ¼ cup water in blender, and blend for 30 seconds, pushing food onto blades if necessary.

2 Add the remaining ¼ cup water, and blend until desired consistency.

CALORIES	FAT	PROTEIN	SODIUM	CARBOHYDRATES	SUGARS	FIBER
95	0 grams	1 gram	3 milligrams	25 grams	19 grams	3 grams

NUTRITION NEWS: *Energy Needs*

Energy for muscle activity comes from both glucose and fat. We are always using fat for energy while at rest; however, during intense exercise, glucose is the main source of energy. As kids burn through their glucose, glycogen, the stored form of glucose, begins to fuel activity. The best way to build up these glycogen stores before exercise is to eat foods high in carbohydrates. Carbohydrates are easily digested and stay in the stomach for a shorter amount of time than fat or protein. Active kids should take in plenty of carbohydrates, and one way to do so is to eat bananas and mangoes.

Melon Melodies

ACTIVE KIDS: Even kids who want to play outside all afternoon begin to drag after a while. This smoothie will give them that pick-me-up they need to keep playing in the yard until dinnertime!

FOUR 1-CUP SERVINGS

1 cup endive

1 cantaloupe, peeled and seeds removed

1 honeydew melon, peeled and seeds removed

1 cup ice

1 Combine all ingredients except ice in a blender, and blend for 30 seconds.

2 Pull the lid off, and give the mixture a quick stir to get all the food to the blades.

3 Add the ice, and blend until appropriate texture is achieved.

CALORIES	FAT	PROTEIN	SODIUM	CARBOHYDRATES	SUGARS	FIBER
141	1 gram	3 grams	67 milligrams	35 grams	31 grams	4 grams

NUTRITION NEWS: Hydration

Dehydration can be dangerous, if not deadly, for young children. Kids are at risk for dehydration if the temperature is hot, they are playing hard outside, they are overworked, their clothes are too tight, they've been sick, they are new to exercise, or they aren't well rested. Dehydration can make a child very sick. Make sure kids take drink breaks often during playing, games, and practice; ensure they are wearing loose clothing; and help them build up the endurance necessary to perform certain tasks.

Banana Bonanza

BRAIN SUPPORT: Energy for school and an improved memory is a great reason to consume walnuts. This smoothie combines the nutty flavor of walnuts with bananas, bringing back memories of eating banana bread for your kids.

FOUR 1-CUP SERVINGS

½ cup walnuts

1 cup vanilla almond milk

1 cup romaine lettuce

2 bananas, peeled

1 Combine all ingredients in a blender, and blend on high for 30 seconds.

2 Open lid to blender, stir down the unprocessed nuts and lettuce, and blend until it has all been incorporated.

CALORIES	FAT	PROTEIN	SODIUM	CARBOHYDRATES	SUGARS	FIBER
183	11 grams	5 grams	33 milligrams	20 grams	10 grams	3 grams

GREEN TIP: Garbage

While snack food and fast-food packaging contribute a large amount to our landfill problem, food waste actually contributes more. One study suggested Americans throw out almost half the total food they bring into their house, produce as well as premade food. Limit a portion of food wasted by blending up all your produce before it expires—that way you don't waste it! Smoothies and juices you just can't quite finish will be delicious the next day by popping them in the freezer for later. Take smoothies and juices out of the freezer when you are ready to drink them again. No need to waste a good drink!

Maggie and the Ferocious Beet

ANTI-INFLAMMATION: This smoothie is designed to combat inflammation resulting in joint and muscle redness or swelling. The high antioxidants in beets and carrots are the perfect anti-inflammatory combination.

FOUR 1-CUP SERVINGS

1 cup beet greens

2 beets, peeled and chopped

2 carrots, peeled

1 cucumber, peeled

2 cups water

1 Take beet greens, beets, carrots, cucumber, and 1 cup water, and place in a blender. Blend until smooth, with beets and carrots chopped finely by the blender.

2 Add remaining water, and blend until completely smooth and there are no foods unprocessed.

CALORIES	FAT	PROTEIN	SODIUM	CARBOHYDRATES	SUGARS	FIBER
45	0 grams	2 grams	80 milligrams	46 grams	6 grams	3 grams

TIME SAVER TIP: Carrot Cubes

For smoothies that include carrots in the recipe, prepare them ahead of time and you'll always have them ready. First, place carrots in a microwave-safe dish. Cover them with water. Cook in the microwave for up to 5 minutes, or until carrots are tender. Drain water and purée the carrots in a blender or food processor. Scoop the puréed carrots into an ice cube tray and freeze. Pop the frozen carrot cubes into a freezer-safe plastic bag. Each time a smoothie recipe calls for carrots and you don't have any fresh ones, use the frozen carrot purée cubes.

Adventure Lime

ANTI-INFLAMMATION: The avocados in this smoothie are not only delicious, but their anti-inflammatory properties are amazing. The fat in avocados increases our bodies' ability to absorb the other nutrients in this smoothie by up to 400 percent.

FOUR 1-CUP SERVINGS

- 1 cup spinach
- 2 avocados, peeled and seed removed
- 1 lime, peeled
- 1 tablespoon agave nectar
- 1 cup water
- 1 cup vegan-style plain yogurt

1 Combine spinach, avocados, lime, agave, and water in a blender, and blend until smooth and creamy.

2 Mix in yogurt with a long spoon, and blend until food is all incorporated. Smoothie will be creamy.

CALORIES	FAT	PROTEIN	SODIUM	CARBOHYDRATES	SUGARS	FIBER
221	17 grams	4 grams	42 milligrams	18 grams	8 grams	7 grams

GREEN TIP: Meatless Mondays

You don't need to be vegetarian to enjoy this vegan smoothie. However, eating a vegetarian lifestyle once a week can benefit your health, the environment, and your pocketbook. Join millions of others and choose a meat-free day, like Mondays, to enjoy this smoothie and have a delicious vegetable soup for dinner. Your kids will reduce their risk for obesity, diabetes, cardiovascular problems, cholesterol, and cancer. As an added benefit, going vegetarian one day a week has been shown to help you live longer! We can all live with that.

Zeus's Zucchini Blend

EYE HEALTH: The combination of zucchini and carrots brings the content of this smoothie's antioxidants to new levels. Both vegetables are excellent sources of manganese, vitamin C, and beta-carotene.

FOUR 1-CUP SERVINGS

1 cup spinach

1 zucchini

3 carrots, peeled

2 red apples, cored and peeled

2 cups water

1 Take spinach, zucchini, carrots, apples, and 1 cup water, and place in blender. Blend for 30 seconds.

2 Slowly stir the mixture, and add the remaining water. Blend until smoothie is the desired consistency.

CALORIES	FAT	PROTEIN	SODIUM	CARBOHYDRATES	SUGARS	FIBER
71	0 grams	2 grams	47 milligrams	17 grams	12 grams	3 grams

TIME SAVER TIP: Shred Zucchini

With zucchini being one of the easiest vegetables to grow, many people find themselves with a large harvest every fall. While giving some zucchini to the neighbors is a great idea, this fall shred some up and save it for the winter. Pick zucchini while they are relatively small, about 12" long or smaller. (When zucchini gets too big, it holds a lot of water, and many large seeds.) Take a standard cheese grater, and shred each zucchini into a pile, including the skin and the seeds. Place 1 cup of shredded zucchini in freezer-safe bags and write the date on the bag. You can use the shredded zucchini for this smoothie (use 1 bag when it calls for 1 zucchini). You can also use the frozen shredded zucchini for zucchini bread or muffins, or even add it to pancakes.

JUICES

The Tomato Tornado Juice

MEMORY: The memory-enhancing benefits of cauliflower, lettuce, and tomatoes in this juice make it the perfect drink to send to school with your little student.

TWO ½-CUP SERVINGS

1 tomato
3 red lettuce leaves
½ cup cauliflower

1 Combine all ingredients in a juicer.

2 Run the juicer until you are able to extract 1 full cup of juice.

CALORIES	FAT	PROTEIN	SODIUM	CARBOHYDRATES	SUGARS	FIBER
23	0 grams	2 grams	21 milligrams	5 grams	2 grams	2 grams

NUTRITION NEWS: Zinc for Memory

Zinc has long been known for its ability to enhance immune systems, but did you know it can also help balance blood sugar levels, stabilize your metabolic rate, and enhance your sense of taste and smell? The most recent studies are also linking zinc to improved memory. This is a bonus for parents who want their kids to have that extra edge in the classroom.

Yummy Yammy Apple Juice

ENERGY SUPPORT: Not just for Thanksgiving, yams are great to have around all year. Families who have trouble with their produce going bad before they have a chance to eat it will be glad to know yams can stay fresh for up to 1 month if stored in a dark, cool environment.

1 CUP

1 yam, peeled and cut
    into pieces
1 red apple, sliced in half

1 Juice both the yam and the apple.

2 Stir together and serve.

CALORIES	FAT	PROTEIN	SODIUM	CARBOHYDRATES	SUGARS	FIBER
77	0 grams	0 grams	0 milligrams	21 grams	16 grams	2 grams

NUTRITION NEWS: Iron and Vitamin C

Iron provides your kids with energy, strengthened immunity, and better concentration! Yams are a good source of iron, which is more easily absorbed by our bodies when it comes from a food source rather than a supplement. The vitamin C in yams assists with the transportation and absorption of the iron. Although yams only have 8 percent of the recommended daily value of iron, our kids actually get more iron out of that vegetable than other sources of iron.

Punchy Peach

SKIN SUPPORT: Vitamin A does more than support good eye health. It can also keep skin and mucous cell membranes healthy. Peaches are packed with vitamin A, so drink up!

THREE ½-CUP SERVINGS

1 cup pineapple, skin removed

1 peach, pitted

1 Place pineapple and pitted peach into a juicer through the input funnel.

2 Turn on juicer, and run until both fruits have been processed.

CALORIES	FAT	PROTEIN	SODIUM	CARBOHYDRATES	SUGARS	FIBER
46	0 grams	1 gram	1 milligram	12 grams	10 grams	2 grams

GREEN TIP: Using Pineapple Juice

Being conscious of the environment and our resources requires us to use up what we produce, rather than dump or waste it. For example, this recipe doesn't require an entire pineapple, just part of one—but don't throw away the extra. Use the rest of the pineapple juice for a teriyaki marinade or other sauce.

Oh-my-a Papaya

DIGESTION: The papaya in this juice is full of digestive enzymes that assist with the digestion of proteins. This diverse enzyme, called papain, has also been shown beneficial in treating sports injuries, trauma, and allergies.

THREE ½-CUP SERVINGS

2 papayas, peeled and seeds removed
1 cup strawberries

1 Push papaya and strawberries into the spout of a juicer, and run through the juicer.

2 Keep the juicer turned on while pushing the food all the way through until the food has been completely juiced.

CALORIES	FAT	PROTEIN	SODIUM	CARBOHYDRATES	SUGARS	FIBER
94	0 grams	2 grams	6 milligrams	23 grams	14 grams	5 grams

MAKE IT FUN: Papaya Boats

Papayas are a gorgeous fruit that can double as a holding container for fruit salads or can even be used as a punch bowl! First, cut a large papaya lengthwise from end to end. Scoop out the seeds from one half with a spoon. Scrape out a little extra flesh to make a deep bowl in the papaya fruit. Use a portion of this flesh to chop for your fruit salad, or juice it for papaya juice. With the seeds scooped out, and the papaya turned into a bowl (or boat), fill it with fruit salad or juice. Serve at your next meal.

Queen Carot-tene

CLEANSING: After a vacation of eating on the road and getting very little sleep, everyone in the house could benefit from the cleansing effects of this carrot-beet juice. The enzymes and nutrients in beet juice assist in the cleansing of the blood, liver, and kidneys.

THREE ½-CUP SERVINGS

3 carrots, peeled
1 cucumber, peeled
1 beet, greens removed

1 Juice the carrots, cucumber, and beet all in one juicer.

2 Collect the juice from all three foods in one container, and stir before serving.

CALORIES	FAT	PROTEIN	SODIUM	CARBOHYDRATES	SUGARS	FIBER
56	0 grams	2 grams	73 milligrams	13 grams	7 grams	3 grams

PICKY EATER: Vegetable Grains

Juicing fresh vegetables is delicious and nutritious. Not all kids, however, are going to be excited about drinking it. There are plenty of ways to get your kids to consume a cup of vegetable juice without their realizing it. You can also use this juice—or any vegetable juice—to make a delicious addition as a replacement for water in cooking whole grains. For example, if you were to cook 1 cup of rice, instead of adding 2 cups of water, use 2 cups of this vegetable juice. Cooking 1 cup of quinoa generally uses 1½ cups of water. Replace this water with 1½ cups of vegetable juice instead. The result is flavorful and delicious!

Melonopolis

*MIGRAINES: For those children who suffer from migraines,
try handing them this smooth and spicy cantaloupe juice.
The ginger in this juice can help ease their symptoms
(see the sidebar with this recipe for more details).*

TWO ½-CUP SERVINGS

½ **cantaloupe, peeled**
¼" **slice fresh
gingerroot**
½ **lemon, peeled**

1 Place cantaloupe, ginger, and lemon in a juicer.

2 Run the juicer, and collect the juice in a single container. Stir together before serving.

CALORIES	FAT	PROTEIN	SODIUM	CARBOHYDRATES	SUGARS	FIBER
60	0 grams	1 gram	23 milligrams	13 grams	11 grams	2 grams

NUTRITION NEWS: Ginger

The anti-inflammatory properties of ginger contribute to its ability to reduce migraine symptoms, as well as relieve symptoms of arthritis pain. A recent study showed that 75–100 percent of patients who consumed ginger regularly found relief from pain, compared to patients being treated with a placebo. Patients who continued to consume ginger found their pain was reduced and remained low for the entire course of the study. Patients who were given a placebo found no relief from their pain.

Cool as a Cucumber

HEART HEALTH: For maximum health and nutrition, don't peel the cucumber this time. The skin contains chlorophyll, a phytonutrient vital to transporting nutrients to muscles and cells.

THREE ½-CUP SERVINGS

1 cucumber

2 cups red sweet cherries, pitted

2 celery stalks, leaves intact

1 Juice the cucumbers, cherries, and then stalks of celery.

2 Collect in a single pitcher, and stir before serving.

CALORIES	FAT	PROTEIN	SODIUM	CARBOHYDRATES	SUGARS	FIBER
84	0 grams	2 grams	23 milligrams	21 grams	15 grams	3 grams

GREEN TIP: Shop Seasonally

Flavor, texture, taste, and total nutrients are all at their best when fruits and vegetables are picked ripe and eaten quickly. Fruits and vegetables that have to travel long distances use more resources, lose nutrients, and lose flavor. The best and most environmentally friendly way to consume fruits and vegetables is to purchase fresh, seasonal, and local produce.

One Leopard's Pepper Drink

IMMUNITY: Even after being picked, as bell peppers get riper their vitamin C content actually increases! While cooking the peppers destroys some of this vitamin C, juicing them won't. So, drink up and stay healthy this winter!

TWO ½-CUP SERVINGS

2 red apples, cored

1 bell pepper

1 Juice the apples and pepper together, and collect in a single container.

2 Stir the juices together, then serve.

CALORIES	FAT	PROTEIN	SODIUM	CARBOHYDRATES	SUGARS	FIBER
89	0 grams	1 gram	2 milligrams	23 grams	18 grams	3 grams

MAKE IT FUN: Pepper Flowers

Cutting peppers across the equator shows off their gorgeous shapes. Cutting a pepper this way, close to the stem, makes it look like a flower. Punch out the center stem, and put a chopped carrot into the hole for your flower's center. Use different color peppers for different colored flowers and arrange on a tray to look like a flower garden. For more flower vegetables, chop two wedges out of a carrot coin to look like a tulip. Insert a toothpick into the bottom of the carrot coin as the flower stem.

The Purple Cow

STRONG BONES: The bone benefits in this drink don't end with calcium in the milk! Both blackberries and blueberries contain small amounts of magnesium and phosphorus that work synergistically to build and maintain bones.

THREE ½-CUP SERVINGS

1 cup blueberries
1 pint blackberries
½ cup skim milk

1 First juice the blueberries and then the blackberries in a juicer, and collect in a single container.

2 Stir the milk into the juice.

CALORIES	FAT	PROTEIN	SODIUM	CARBOHYDRATES	SUGARS	FIBER
103	1 gram	4 grams	23 milligrams	20 grams	12 grams	7 grams

NUTRITION NEWS: Vitamin D and Bone Health

Both osteoporosis and osteopenia, diseases characterized by bone weakening, are becoming more and more common despite an increase in the amount of calcium in our diets. Researchers have begun taking a look at the impact of vitamin D on bone health and its role in bone development. Also referred to as the "sunshine vitamin," vitamin D regulates the absorption and excretion of calcium and phosphorus. When our calcium levels are low, vitamin D allows us to absorb more calcium from our food. When our calcium levels are high, we absorb less calcium during digestion. Without vitamin D, this process couldn't be regulated, and we would possibly be deficient in important bone-building calcium, even when our diets are rich with it.

Sweet Swiss Sipper

BLOOD SUGAR CONTROL: As far as superfoods are concerned, Swiss chard may as well be the queen. Second only in nutrient density to spinach, Swiss chard is packed with blood-sugar-stabilizing nutrients. Adding orange juice to Swiss chard gives kids the nutrients they need with the enjoyable, familiar flavors of orange juice.

TWO ½-CUP SERVINGS

2 large oranges, peeled

2 Swiss chard leaves

1 Juices the oranges and leaves of the Swiss chard through a juicer.

2 Collect juice in a single container, and stir before serving.

CALORIES	FAT	PROTEIN	SODIUM	CARBOHYDRATES	SUGARS	FIBER
71	0 grams	2 grams	102 milligrams	17 grams	13 grams	4 grams

NUTRITION NEWS: Swiss Chard

With fiber, protein, enzymes, phytonutrients, and antioxidants all contained in a single leaf of Swiss chard, you will want your kids to have this vegetable in their diets. Studies have shown that when you eat Swiss chard following a meal, your blood sugar levels from that meal remain steady. A specific enzyme in the Swiss chard seems to control the amount of carbohydrates broken down from the meal, allowing you to avoid the dips and spikes of less-controlled carbohydrate breakdown. The fiber and protein in Swiss chard both have properties that slow digestion, meaning the glucose from the meal is released more slowly into the bloodstream instead of hitting it all at once.

Butternut Bug Juice

BRAIN FUNCTION: This juice tastes so much like pumpkin juice, you wouldn't believe there is no pumpkin in it. Butternut squash is a great source of folate, a brain-healthy nutrient.

TWO ½-CUP SERVINGS

2 Gala apples, cored
½ butternut squash, peeled and cut into pieces
1 teaspoon pumpkin pie spice

1 Juice the apples and squash into a single cup or pitcher.

2 Stir in the pumpkin pie spice, and serve warm. For every 1 cup of juice, warm in the microwave for 30 seconds on high. Mix thoroughly so there are no hot spots.

CALORIES	FAT	PROTEIN	SODIUM	CARBOHYDRATES	SUGARS	FIBER
77	0 grams	0 grams	0 milligrams	21 grams	16 grams	2 grams

NUTRITION NEWS: Folate

The dietary supplement folic acid has been enriched into many foods this past decade as an attempt to make sure our diets were not deficient in this brain-supporting nutrient. Folate, the natural form of folic acid, is present mostly in green leafy vegetables, but it's also in winter squashes, such as butternut squash. During periods of growth, folate is essential. Children, teenagers, and pregnant mothers all need folate in their diet to build DNA and form new cells. Folate deficiencies lead to weakness, irritability, diarrhea, and anemia.

Groovy Grape Juice

HEART HEALTH: While high cholesterol and high blood pressure generally aren't an issue for young children, instilling the habits that will keep their hearts strong is! Teach kids to love grape juice, and their bodies will thank them for keeping their arteries clean.

THREE ½-CUP SERVINGS

1 cup red grapes
1 cup pineapple
1 cup strawberries, hulls intact

1 Juice the grapes, pineapple, and strawberries into a single container.

2 Stir the juices together, and then pour into individual cups.

CALORIES	FAT	PROTEIN	SODIUM	CARBOHYDRATES	SUGARS	FIBER
78	0 grams	1 gram	2 milligrams	20 grams	16 grams	2 grams

NUTRITION NEWS: Flavonoids

Flavonoids are a variety of compounds that may carry out antiviral, antiallergic, antiplatelet, antitumor, and antioxidant activities. Dark purple grapes and berries are full of these flavonoids. Frequent colds or flu, nose bleeds, swelling, or bruising can be an indicator a child is not consuming enough high-flavonoid foods. While the heat of cooking destroys some of the total flavonoids contained in a food, juicing preserves them. Juicing dark red grapes is a great way to get these important flavonoids each day.

Pink PJ Pineapple

ENERGY: This pineapple-papaya-strawberry juice is full of B vitamins, a necessary cofactor for energy production and synthesis. Drinking this juice just before a soccer game or a family bike ride will give kids adequate carbs and vitamins for the energy they need.

THREE ½-CUP SERVINGS

1 cup strawberries

1 cup pineapple, flesh only

1 papaya, seeded

1 Combine strawberries, pineapple, and papaya in a juicer, and juice.

2 Collect into a single cup or bowl, and stir until all juices are combined.

CALORIES	FAT	PROTEIN	SODIUM	CARBOHYDRATES	SUGARS	FIBER
54	0 grams	1 gram	4 milligrams	14 grams	8 grams	3 grams

GREEN TIP: *Juice Repurpose*

This juice can be used and reused for many different drinks. Keep some juice, then add ice and yogurt for a creamy smoothie. Use some of the juice to freeze and then grind up for a tropical slushy treat. Save some of the juice to mix into pancake batter, instead of water, for some tropical pancakes. Use some of the juice to sprinkle over fruit salad to keep fruit salad from going brown. Take any leftover juice, and pour into popsicle molds for an afternoon refreshment.

Taste Beyond Be-Leaf

MEMORY: The folate in these greens contains a much-needed nutrient for kids and pregnant moms. Folate provides support to keep memory sharp and protect it from deteriorating, something pregnant women know all too much about!

THREE ½-CUP SERVINGS

1 red apple, cut in half
4 romaine lettuce
   leaves
1 cucumber, peeled
1 celery stalk, leaves
   intact
1 carrot, peeled

1 Push apple, lettuce, cucumber, celery, and carrot, one at a time, into the funnel of a juicer.

2 Juice entire ingredients, combine into one pitcher, and stir.

CALORIES	FAT	PROTEIN	SODIUM	CARBOHYDRATES	SUGARS	FIBER
33	0 grams	1 gram	32 milligrams	7 grams	3 grams	2 grams

NUTRITION NEWS: New USDA Icon

In 1992, the USDA introduced a pyramid to illustrate the dietary guidelines. Owing to concerns registered by nutritionists and others, the pyramid was replaced in 2011 with a plate graphic, illustrating to the public that half our meals should be fruits and vegetables. This new graphic is easy to understand and will help people put into practice the dietary guidelines. Juices and smoothies, while in a glass rather than on a plate, are a great way to meet dietary needs.

The O.C. Specialty

HEART HEALTH: Packed with antioxidants and phytochemicals, oranges and carrots can keep arteries clean, prevent plaque buildup, and prevent damage to the fragile cardiovascular system. This juice tastes so much like an already familiar juice, orange juice, that the kids won't even know it's also good for them.

TWO ½-CUP SERVINGS

1 orange, peeled

3 carrots

1 Put the orange and carrots into the intake funnel of a juicer.

2 Run the juicer until you've extracted as much juice as possible.

CALORIES	FAT	PROTEIN	SODIUM	CARBOHYDRATES	SUGARS	FIBER
75	0 grams	2 grams	74 milligrams	18 grams	11 grams	5 grams

PICKY EATER: Give Kids Options

For some kitchen fun that even the pickiest eater will want to try, let your kids mix their own juices. Juice fruits and vegetables separately and put each juice in a labeled glass. For different, fun colors, use orange, celery, blackberries, grapes, lettuce, and lemons. Set out empty glasses and tablespoons, and let them mix their own drinks. They can use a tablespoon of "this" and a tablespoon of "that" until they have a glass full of juice. They can try their own drinks and each other's drinks. The ownership they'll have over making their own drinks is enough to have some of the pickiest drinkers enjoying what they created themselves.

Tooty Fruity Grapefruit Juicy

DIVERSITY: Juicing grapefruit is a great way to introduce new flavors to your kids. The tangy tartness of grapefruits gives this juice a different flavor than the sweet juices they are used to.

TWO 1-CUP SERVINGS

3 red apples
1 pink grapefruit, peeled

1 Juice apples and grapefruit.

2 Mix together thoroughly. Stir once more before drinking.

CALORIES	FAT	PROTEIN	SODIUM	CARBOHYDRATES	SUGARS	FIBER
156	0 grams	1 gram	0 milligrams	41 grams	33 grams	4 grams

NUTRITION NEWS: Choose Pink

Beta-carotene, a dietary carotenoid that can be converted to useful vitamin A, is found in grapefruit. Whereas a whole white grapefruit only contains 14 mcg of beta-carotene, pink and red grapefruits contain 384 mcg. Vitamin A is important in promoting healthy vision, immunity, and skin.

Kaleade

MULTIVITAMIN: The first time we made this with my four-year-old niece, she tried to stop us because she exclaimed leaves were only for bugs to eat. Once she realized humans should eat leaves, too, she was hooked.

ONE 1-CUP SERVING

2 Granny Smith apples
3 kale leaves

1 Juice apples and kale.

2 Mix thoroughly and enjoy.

CALORIES	FAT	PROTEIN	SODIUM	CARBOHYDRATES	SUGARS	FIBER
196	1 gram	4 grams	36 milligrams	49 grams	32 grams	6 grams

NUTRITION NEWS: Balanced Diet

The list of nutrients in kale is extensive, and the micronutrients, minerals, and antioxidants it contains are some of the highest in the vegetable kingdom. But did you know kale also has a perfect balance of macronutrients? One cup of kale contains 7 grams of carbohydrates, 2.5 grams of protein, 0.5 grams of healthy fat, and 2.6 grams of fiber, all for only 34 calories. This is a great drink for those kids who get stuck in a food rut, where it's difficult to get them to eat a variety of food. The variety is in the kale!

Easy Peasy Grapefruit Squeezy

IMMUNITY: This juice is full of vitamin C to strengthen your kids' immune system and get them ready for winter. Temper the tart taste of grapefruit with oranges, ginger, and cucumber. What you get is a refreshing drink without the sour face.

THREE ½-CUP SERVINGS

1 pink grapefruit, peeled
1 orange, peeled
¼" slice ginger
1 cucumber, peeled

1 Juice the grapefruit, orange, ginger, and cucumber into a single pitcher.

2 Stir the juices together until well combined.

CALORIES	FAT	PROTEIN	SODIUM	CARBOHYDRATES	SUGARS	FIBER
65	0 grams	2 grams	2 milligrams	16 grams	12 grams	3 grams

MAKE IT FUN: Juicing on Vacation

It may be tempting to leave your juicer home when you go on vacation, but nothing could be better! Heading to new places gives your family a new opportunity to try new, fresh, and local produce that you may not be able to get where you live or that may not taste as fresh and delicious. Next time you head to Florida on vacation, bring your juicer and get some local grapefruit and oranges. Try to take your kids to orchards where these are grown. With your fresh fruit, make this juice and see if your kids can tell any difference in taste. Drinking fresh juice on vacation is a great way to stay healthy and enjoy your vacation even more.

Carrotopia

MOTION SICKNESS: Including ginger is a natural way to calm irritated bellies. Some kids get sick driving just across town or getting on the school bus for a short drive. Don't let them arrive at school feeling lousy. Have them drink some of this juice before getting on the bus.

ONE ½-CUP SERVING

2 apples, cored
1 carrot, peeled
¼" slice of ginger

1 Juice apples, carrot, and ginger into a single container.

2 Stir juices together until thoroughly mixed.

CALORIES	FAT	PROTEIN	SODIUM	CARBOHYDRATES	SUGARS	FIBER
189	1 gram	2 grams	51 milligrams	49 grams	36 grams	6 grams

PICKY EATER: Various Uses for Ginger

Ginger packs such nutrition that it's worth the effort to ensure your kids get it in their diets. For picky eaters, adding ginger to smoothies, starting with small amounts at a time, is a great way to introduce the food. You can also add ginger to stir-fries and soups. You can also make ginger ale by adding sparkling water to this juice recipe.

Great Grapes and Berries

ANTI-INFLAMMATION: Ulcers, joint pain, or diabetes, whatever the inflammation is responsible for, dark blue and purple foods contain vital antioxidants that help fight and prevent an inflammatory reaction.

TWO ½-CUP SERVINGS

2 cups blueberries, washed

2 cups red grapes, washed

1 Juice the blueberries and the grapes, and collect in a single cup or pitcher.

2 Stir the juices together until flavors are well mixed.

CALORIES	FAT	PROTEIN	SODIUM	CARBOHYDRATES	SUGARS	FIBER
240	2 grams	4 grams	16 milligrams	55 grams	37 grams	7 grams

NUTRITION NEWS: Anthocyanin

The dark purple and blue pigments in fruits and vegetables are a sign they contain an antioxidant called anthocyanin. This antioxidant has many known health benefits. This includes the ability to scavenge and trap free radicals that damage cells. As a result, kids will have less inflammation that leads to disease and pain. Other benefits that have been studied include less risk of obesity, lower blood pressure, and improved lipid levels. Other blue and purple foods that contain this antioxidant include blackberries, red cabbage, red onions, and plums.

Cowabunga Cucumber

ANTICANCER: Research surrounding the nutrient cucurbitacin is showing this phytonutrient can be helpful in preventing cancer. While more research needs to be done, the health benefits are undeniable.

ONE ⅓-CUP SERVING

2 cucumbers
2 lemons, peeled
¼" slice ginger

1 Juice the cucumber, lemons, and ginger into a single glass.

2 Stir well and filter juice through a common coffee filter until juice is consistency kids desire.

CALORIES	FAT	PROTEIN	SODIUM	CARBOHYDRATES	SUGARS	FIBER
65	1 gram	3 grams	8 milligrams	17 grams	7 grams	3 grams

NUTRITION NEWS: Great Skin

While both lemons and cucumbers have been shown to have anticancer properties, there are other benefits as well. Both foods also contain nutrients that enhance and hydrate skin. The vitamin C and citric acid encourage cell turnover, as well as prevent oxidation that leads to aging. This is great for those young kids who have lost the supple and pliable skin they once had as babies.

Cabbage Patch Kids Juice

DIGESTION: Cabbage is an inexpensive yet nutrient-packed filler for this apple juice. The subtle flavors of cabbage are enhanced by the sweet flavors of the apples. Kids will love the juice as much as they love their apple juice.

THREE ½-CUP SERVINGS

¼ head red cabbage
1 cup Napa cabbage
2 Granny Smith apples, cored

1 Juice the cabbages and then the apples, and collect into a single bowl or cup.

2 Stir the juices together well, and chill before serving.

CALORIES	FAT	PROTEIN	SODIUM	CARBOHYDRATES	SUGARS	FIBER
74	0 grams	2 grams	16 milligrams	19 grams	14 grams	4 grams

NUTRITION NEWS: School Lunch

The school lunch landscape is changing. For years, schools have been required to purchase frozen foods from large manufacturers to meet the needs of the children in their districts. Parents, school officials, and health educators are beginning to see the health and academic benefits of providing fresh foods to hungry students. You can do your part by helping your local school plant a school garden, applying for health food grants, introducing kids to new fruits and vegetables, or soliciting donations to improve the options in your school's cafeteria. Until changes are made to your satisfaction, be sure you are sending plenty of fruits and veggies in your own child's lunch box. Send fresh fruit juices in insulated containers to keep them cold and fresh.

Tomato Twister

STRONG BONES: While we mostly think of dairy as beneficial to bone health, tomatoes actually play a large role in bone health as well. Rather than a bone builder, the antioxidants in tomatoes prevent bone loss and deterioration. Because kids are still growing and building bones, their bodies need all the bone health support they can get.

TWO ½-CUP SERVINGS

1 cucumber, peeled
1 Roma tomato

1 Juice the cucumber and the tomato into a single container.

2 Stir the juices well, and chill before serving.

CALORIES	FAT	PROTEIN	SODIUM	CARBOHYDRATES	SUGARS	FIBER
34	0 grams	2 grams	6 milligrams	8 grams	4 grams	1 gram

PICKY EATER: Tomato Soup

Some children may not enjoy drinking tomato juice, but many kids like tomato soup! Simply heat up this juice and add some seasonings such as basil, onions, and cloves. Serve soup with warm whole-wheat rolls for dipping. Squirt a small amount of sour cream on the top, or crumble up tortilla chips. Serving tomato soup every week for lunch will help kids begin to enjoy the flavors of tomato soup, and slowly they will begin to also enjoy tomato juice.

5

Just for Fun (and Then Some):

DRINKS FOR DESSERT

Desserts have become something we eat daily, rather than on special occasions. Unfortunately, our kids are growing up to believe they need something sweet daily. While we could try to retrain them, society is definitely fighting us on this one. Instead of teaching kids they don't need something sweet daily, teach them they can have something sweet but that it can also be beneficial and helpful to their overall health and vitality, rather than detrimental.

Smoothies and juices for dessert can be served at birthday parties, family parties, holidays, or even just after dinner. Replacing sodas, ice cream, or sugar-filled juices with healthy smoothies or juices for these celebrations may even help to control the excitability often associated with kids and parties.

With dessert being typically given at the end of the day, this can also be an opportunity for parents to fill in nutritional gaps. Kids who may not have eaten much during the day, or left broccoli on their dinner plate, can still get fruits and vegetables for dessert.

SMOOTHIES

Peary Punch

This green-colored smoothie is perfect for a little kid's army or camo party. Kids will still drink it up even with the spinach because of the sweetness of the smoothie. Extra bonus: no kids running wild on a sugar high.

TWO 1-CUP SERVINGS

½ cup spinach

2 pears, peeled and cored

1 banana, frozen and peeled

½ cup soy milk or low-fat milk

3 or 4 ice cubes

1 Combine all ingredients in a blender.

2 Mix until well incorporated.

3 Serve.

CALORIES	FAT	PROTEIN	SODIUM	CARBOHYDRATES	SUGARS	FIBER
122	1 gram	3 grams	37 milligrams	27 grams	16 grams	5 grams

NUTRITION NEWS: Not Just for Popeye

Although Popeye was the one to bring attention to the muscle-building benefits of spinach, there are many more reasons to eat spinach that he didn't share. Calorie for calorie, spinach is actually higher in protein than most other vegetables. This is important to provide the necessary nutrients for growing kids.

Banana Split Smoothie

Perfect as an after-dinner treat, this chocolate smoothie hits the spot. Adding honey to smoothies changes kids' perception of it being a drink for health to a dessert drink. What they may not realize, however, is although this dessert smoothie tastes like ice cream, the honey used to sweeten it comes packed with B vitamins.

TWO 1-CUP SERVINGS

8 ounces soy milk or
  low-fat milk
1 tablespoon honey
2 bananas (frozen)
1 tablespoon cocoa
  powder

1 Place milk, honey, frozen bananas, and cocoa powder in a blender, and blend.

2 Serve.

CALORIES	FAT	PROTEIN	SODIUM	CARBOHYDRATES	SUGARS	FIBER
204	3 grams	6 grams	59 milligrams	44 grams	28 grams	5 grams

NUTRITION NEWS: The Power of Cocoa

Cocoa powder is an ingredient with amazing benefits for children. The antioxidants in cocoa powder can help kids have healthier skin, combat diarrhea, improve insulin sensitivity, soothe a cough, plus improve visual as well as verbal memory!

Strawberry Short-Shake

This drink is creamy as a strawberry milkshake, but it's healthy as a dinner salad! Serving this salad-in-a-glass is perfect for those kids who won't eat their vegetables for dinner but love them for dessert.

FOUR 1-CUP SERVINGS

½ cup dandelion greens
2 pints strawberries
2 cups vanilla soy milk
4 or 5 ice cubes
1 tablespoon agave nectar or honey

1 Blend dandelion greens, strawberries, soy milk, and ice in a blender.

2 Add agave or honey, and blend again.

3 If necessary, continue to add soy milk until texture is smooth.

CALORIES	FAT	PROTEIN	SODIUM	CARBOHYDRATES	SUGARS	FIBER
116	3 grams	5 grams	100 milligrams	20 grams	12 grams	4 grams

PICKY EATER: Sweeteners

Sweetening up a dessert smoothie for those picky eaters can also be beneficial. Agave nectar and honey are natural alternatives to more refined and processed sugars. Plus, agave and honey come with the added benefit of vitamins and minerals. Agave contains trace minerals of calcium, potassium, magnesium, and iron. Honey also contains trace minerals and is packed with B vitamins.

Apple Pie in the Sky

Serve this dessert smoothie as written, or add 2 cups ice cubes to the blender to turn it into a milkshake.

FOUR 1-CUP SERVINGS

2 cups spinach
1 teaspoon ground cloves
1 teaspoon ground cinnamon
3 apples, peeled and cored
1½ cups coconut milk

1 Add spinach, spices, and apples to the blender.

2 Pour coconut milk over the top.

3 Blend until smoothie is smooth and the spinach and apples are no longer visible.

CALORIES	FAT	PROTEIN	SODIUM	CARBOHYDRATES	SUGARS	FIBER
105	5 grams	1 gram	24 milligrams	17 grams	12 grams	2 grams

DIY: Storage Tips for Cloves

When looking to purchase cloves for your spice pantry, buying ground cloves isn't necessarily the way to go. Save money by purchasing whole cloves and grind them yourself. Whole cloves can stay fresh for up to a year, whereas ground cloves lose their flavor after just six months. More nutrients are found in cloves that are freshly ground. Nutrients are lost when ground cloves are sitting on a shelf. Check to make sure your cloves are fresh by squeezing them. If a small amount of oil is released, they are still potent. Store your whole cloves in a sealed container in a cool, dark place.

Cuckoo for Coconuts

Invite the grandparents over for a luau-themed dinner party, and serve this tropical drink for dessert. Make your own fresh flower leis and grass skirts, and serve this smoothie in the coconut shells.

FOUR 1-CUP SERVINGS

½ cup almonds
2 cups coconut milk
1 cup romaine lettuce
Flesh of 2 coconuts
1 banana, peeled

1 Put the almonds and 1 cup coconut milk in blender.

2 Blend until almonds are no longer chunky.

3 Add the rest of the coconut milk, the romaine lettuce, the coconut flesh, and the banana.

4 Blend again until smooth.

CALORIES	FAT	PROTEIN	SODIUM	CARBOHYDRATES	SUGARS	FIBER
192	15 grams	3 grams	18 milligrams	13 grams	5 grams	3 grams

TIME SAVER TIP: Freezing Coconut Flesh

Most kids never have a chance to see the outside of a coconut, so they enjoy the discovery of watching you crack open a coconut and scrape the flesh out. However, this is time-consuming! This quick tip is to scrape once and use often. Spend some weekend time opening and scraping out the meat of the coconut, and put the scraps in a freezer-safe container. Keep the coconut flesh in the freezer until you are ready to use it in a smoothie. Preparation for smoothies that call for coconut is a breeze when you have some ready in the freezer!

Powder Puff Pink Punch

High in protein, this pink party smoothie just might be the only protein kids eat on party day. Many kids have never tasted tofu, and this sweet, delicious smoothie is the perfect introduction to it.

FOUR ½-CUP SERVINGS

4 ounces silken tofu
1 cup pomegranate juice
1 cup frozen blackberries

Place all ingredients in a blender, and blend until smoothie is desired consistency.

CALORIES	FAT	PROTEIN	SODIUM	CARBOHYDRATES	SUGARS	FIBER
66	1 gram	3 grams	16 milligrams	12 grams	10 grams	2 grams

NUTRITION NEWS: Pomegranate Juice

One reason pomegranate juice is a nutritional star is because it is so high in antioxidants. Antioxidants stabilize free radicals that damage cell membranes. Pomegranate juice has been shown to improve blood circulation, reduce the risk for heart disease, and even clean plaque already present in arteries. Some studies have shown pomegranate juice alleviates depression, as well as improves bone mass. With all these amazing benefits, adding pomegranate juice to any smoothie is a great idea.

Munchkins Pumpkin Pie

Spending time baking pumpkin pie won't be necessary when you can drink this pumpkin pie smoothie. Serve this at your next Thanksgiving feast, and your kids will find plenty of room for more.

FOUR 1-CUP SERVINGS

- ½ cup pumpkin, cubed or diced
- 1 cup vanilla soy milk
- 1 cup romaine lettuce
- 1 teaspoon cloves
- 1 tablespoon ginger, grated
- 1 teaspoon cinnamon
- ½ cup Greek-style yogurt

1 Blend pumpkin and soy milk in a high-powered blender.

2 Add romaine lettuce, spices, and yogurt to blender. Blend again until smooth.

CALORIES	FAT	PROTEIN	SODIUM	CARBOHYDRATES	SUGARS	FIBER
62	1 gram	5 grams	45 milligrams	8 grams	4 grams	1 gram

NUTRITION NEWS: Pumpkin Seeds

After using the flesh of a pumpkin to whip up delicious smoothies, roast the pumpkin seeds for a powerful boost of nutrients. The seeds are a great source of zinc, which is a mineral that is hard to get through diet. Zinc is vital for immune function and powerful enough to fight common bugs. Break open the seed from the hull and eat the small seed inside, rather than the whole thing! The hull will provide you with fiber but is often tough to chew.

Maple Almond Crush

This smoothie dessert includes maple syrup as a sweetener. True maple syrup has naturally occurring zinc and manganese, which not only can support immunity but also promote enzyme activity. This is healthy living, disguised as dessert.

FOUR ½-CUP SERVINGS

1 cup vanilla yogurt
1 cup crushed ice
½ teaspoon almond extract
1 tablespoon maple syrup
¼ cup almonds

1 Place yogurt, ice, almond extract, and maple syrup in a blender, and blend until smooth.

2 Add the almonds and re-blend, just until combined and creamy.

CALORIES	FAT	PROTEIN	SODIUM	CARBOHYDRATES	SUGARS	FIBER
101	4 grams	4 grams	44 milligrams	14 grams	9 grams	1 gram

DIY: Tap Your Own Syrup

Have any maple trees in your yard? You can actually collect your own maple syrup. Harvest season generally runs from February to March. For about 4–6 weeks when the evening temperatures are freezing and the daytime temperatures are starting to warm up, the sap flows freely and is easy to capture. A sugar maple tree that has a diameter of 12" or more is ideal for syrup. With a drill, drill a hole about 2–3 inches deep. Insert a spile (a spike with a hollow center) to allow the sap to flow freely from the tree, and collect your syrup in a bucket. Yum, yum!

Banana Boat Float

*For optimal digestion, probiotics, and a complete protein source,
this banana smoothie contains kefir instead of regular yogurt.
If your family hasn't tried kefir, this is the perfect introduction.*

FOUR 1-CUP SERVINGS

1 cup spinach
2 pints strawberries
1 banana, peeled
1 cup kefir

1 Combine spinach, strawberries, banana, and
kefir in a blender.

2 Blend until smooth.

CALORIES	FAT	PROTEIN	SODIUM	CARBOHYDRATES	SUGARS	FIBER
108	1 gram	5 grams	54 milligrams	23 grams	15 grams	4 grams

GREEN TIP: Repurpose Strawberry Containers

Gone are the days when you can purchase strawberries in cute little baskets. We
mostly see strawberries sold in clear plastic clam shell containers. These containers don't need to go straight to the trash. Use a container to pack a lunch,
grow a plant, return them to the market for reuse, put cookies in and bring to a
neighbor, store small toys, or hold crayons or games with small pieces.

Triple Berry Blastoff

*Triple the berries for triple the antioxidants, triple the vitamins,
and triple the delicious flavor. Including romaine lettuce adds
almost 100 percent of your vitamin K intake for the day.*

FOUR 1-CUP SERVINGS

1 cup romaine lettuce
1 pint blueberries
1 pint raspberries
2 pints strawberries
2 bananas, peeled
1 cup vanilla almond
    milk
1 cup Greek-style yogurt

1 Combine lettuce, blueberries, raspberries, strawberries, bananas, and vanilla almond milk in a blender, and blend until smooth.

2 Add Greek-style yogurt, and blend until thoroughly mixed.

CALORIES	FAT	PROTEIN	SODIUM	CARBOHYDRATES	SUGARS	FIBER
267	3 grams	12 grams	64 milligrams	52 grams	29 grams	12 grams

DIY: Freezing Strawberries

There is no question, freezing your own strawberries is a money saver. You can grow your own, or head over to a local picking farm. First, cut the stems out of your unwashed strawberries. Make sure strawberries are completely dry. Lay them on a wax-paper–lined cookie sheet, and freeze them for 2–4 hours, until they begin to be firm. This way the strawberries will freeze separately and not in one big clump. Then, scoop all the strawberries into a freezer-safe bag for storing in the freezer. They will last 10–12 months.

Queen Cocoa Bean

Top this dessert smoothie with some whipping cream and shaved chocolate pieces. You and your children won't know the difference between this healthy chocolate smoothie and a creamy restaurant shake.

FOUR 1-CUP SERVINGS

- 1 cup romaine lettuce
- 2 bananas, peeled
- 1 tablespoon raw cocoa powder
- ½ vanilla bean pulp or 1 teaspoon vanilla extract
- 2 cups almond milk

1 Take romaine lettuce, bananas, cocoa powder, vanilla bean pulp (or vanilla extract), and 1 cup almond milk, and place in a blender. Blend until smooth.

2 Open blender lid, and slowly pour in the remaining 1 cup almond milk until the texture is desirable.

CALORIES	FAT	PROTEIN	SODIUM	CARBOHYDRATES	SUGARS	FIBER
123	3 grams	5 grams	64 milligrams	22 grams	2 grams	3 grams

GREEN TIP: Saving Energy

Running a blender takes energy. With this recipe, double the batch and save some for later. You will save on power by not running the blender daily, and save on water by only washing the blender container once. This smoothie is perfect for storing extra in the refrigerator. Just give it a good shake before drinking it later. Store this recipe in the freezer and eat it as ice cream later. Take out of the freezer 15 minutes early, and it will soften sufficiently for scooping. This smoothie, when frozen, tastes just like chocolate ice cream!

Radical Raspberry Delight

At your next family gathering, leave the soda and ice cream home and whip up a few batches of this smoothie. Pour all of it into a big punch bowl with a deep ladle and add fresh lemon slices on top.

FOUR 1-CUP SERVINGS

1 cup raspberries

½ pineapple, peeled and cored

½ lemon, peeled

1½ cups kefir

1 Place raspberries, pineapple, lemon, and 1 cup kefir in a blender, and mix.

2 Continue to blend while adding the remaining ½ cup kefir. Process until smooth.

CALORIES	FAT	PROTEIN	SODIUM	CARBOHYDRATES	SUGARS	FIBER
91	0 grams	3 grams	25 milligrams	22 grams	15 grams	4 grams

GREEN TIP: Lemons

Use the other half of the lemon for cleaning around the house. Lemons are acidic and can help cut grease like a household cleaner. Squeeze ½ of a lemon into a squirt bottle filled with water. Use to clean counters, bathrooms, inside the fridge, and inside the microwave. Not only will your house smell good, but your lemon won't be wasted, and the cleaning solution is safe for kids.

Pee-Wee's Kiwi Crush

Use half of a lemon for this delicious smoothie, and use the other half of the lemon for party decorations. Float half a lemon in a shallow vase with some yellow and blue hydrangeas floating with it. Serve the smoothie on the table alongside the centerpiece.

FOUR 1-CUP SERVINGS

2 cups mangoes, peeled and pitted
2 tangerines, peeled
4 kiwis, peeled
½ lemon, peeled
2 cups water

1 Combine mangoes, tangerines, kiwis, lemon, and 1 cup water in a blender, and blend thoroughly, about 30 seconds.

2 Add remaining 1 cup water, and blend again for at least 60 seconds or until fruit is completely smooth.

CALORIES	FAT	PROTEIN	SODIUM	CARBOHYDRATES	SUGARS	FIBER
131	1 gram	2 grams	7 milligrams	33 grams	18 grams	5 grams

NUTRITION NEWS: Water

With many types of water to choose from—tap water, distilled water, filtered, bottled—it can be overwhelming to decide which is best. Each type of water has its pros and cons, so ultimately it's a personal choice. Tap water is free and regulated to control harmful substances, but your city may allow things in your water that you aren't comfortable with, like fluoride. Distilled water tastes great, but vital minerals have been filtered out of it. Filtered water tastes great, retains some important minerals, but may be pricey. Bottled water is convenient, but it is less regulated and is generally a mystery as to what is in it without testing it in a lab. Throwing away the plastic bottles is also harmful to the environment. So, ultimately, it's up to you. All the smoothies in this book taste great with any water you choose.

Spin-erry Canary

Using bananas in this smoothie adds a creaminess that is reminiscent of ice cream, without the dairy. With the cherries and spinach, you'll have no trouble letting your kids have this "ice cream" for breakfast.

FOUR 1-CUP SERVINGS

1 cup spinach
2 cups cherries, pitted
2 bananas, peeled
½ lemon, peeled
2 cups almond milk

1 Take spinach, cherries, bananas, lemon, and 1 cup almond milk, and place in blender to blend.

2 Blend until ingredients are well combined.

3 Add the remaining 1 cup almond milk, and blend until drink is smooth.

CALORIES	FAT	PROTEIN	SODIUM	CARBOHYDRATES	SUGARS	FIBER
170	3 grams	6 grams	69 milligrams	34 grams	22 grams	4 grams

MAKE IT FUN: Cherry-Pit-Spitting Contest

When making this smoothie for your next party, save some cherries for an extra-fun game. Put a bowl full of cherries in the yard for a cherry-pit-spitting contest. Kids love this game! Once they figure out how to put the cherry in their mouth, remove the fruit, and not swallow the pit, they can play along. Flag how far one kid can spit a pit with posts or flags, and give the winner his or her own bag of cherries to take home!

Agua Melon Fresca

Although seedless watermelon is available for purchase, black seeds in watermelon are safe to eat. Return black seeds to the top of your smoothie and your drink will look like a ladybug.

FOUR 1-CUP SERVINGS

2 cups watermelon, seeds and rind removed

2 bananas, peeled

1 cup plain yogurt

1 cup ice

1 Combine watermelon, bananas, and yogurt in a blender, and blend until smooth.

2 Add ice if desired, and blend until smoothie is the consistency desired.

CALORIES	FAT	PROTEIN	SODIUM	CARBOHYDRATES	SUGARS	FIBER
112	2 grams	3 grams	30 milligrams	22 grams	15 grams	2 grams

GREEN TIP: Make Vegetables the Star

The amount of energy to produce one pound of fruits or vegetables versus one pound of meat is significantly less. For minimizing the carbon footprint from your family, consider more fruits and vegetables for your meals as a way to cut back on energy expended to produce your food. Anytime you can have a salad be the star of your dinner, or a smoothie be the focus of your breakfast, you'll be saving energy. Fruit and vegetable smoothies are a great way to replace a high-energy-consuming meal with a low one.

Berry Berry Quite Contrary

This creamy blueberry smoothie tastes great as a drink or frozen like ice cream. Scoop out the frozen smoothie onto an ice cream cone and top with fresh blueberries.

FOUR 1-CUP SERVINGS

1 cup watercress
2 pints blueberries
2 bananas, peeled
1 cup blueberry yogurt
1 cup ice

1 Place watercress, blueberries, bananas, and ½ cup yogurt in a blender, and blend until combined.

2 Add the remaining ½ cup yogurt and the ice, and turn the blender on high for 60 seconds. If all the ingredients are not thoroughly combined, keep blending until it's the desired consistency.

CALORIES	FAT	PROTEIN	SODIUM	CARBOHYDRATES	SUGARS	FIBER
227	4 grams	6 grams	46 milligrams	44 grams	25 grams	7 grams

PICKY EATER: Make Healthy Eating a Family Affair

Kids like to be involved, feel accepted, and feel like they are part of a team. Commit to becoming members of team Healthy Family! Everyone drinks their smoothies, everyone walks together, everyone eats dinner together, and everyone gets plenty of sleep. Being part of the Healthy Family team should be something to be proud of.

Vanilla Banana Bonkers

*Drizzle a small amount of chocolate on top of this smoothie,
then add whipped cream and a cherry. Your kids won't notice
there is no added sugar, and you'll be glad there isn't.*

FOUR ½-CUP SERVINGS

1 cup romaine lettuce
4 bananas, peeled
Pulp of 1½ vanilla beans
   or 1½ teaspoons
   vanilla extract
2 cups vanilla kefir
1 cup ice

1 Place lettuce, bananas, vanilla bean (or vanilla
extract), and vanilla kefir in a blender. Blend
on high speed until smooth.

2 Add 1 cup ice to blender, and blend again until
smoothie is the desired consistency.

CALORIES	FAT	PROTEIN	SODIUM	CARBOHYDRATES	SUGARS	FIBER
175	1 gram	8 grams	96 milligrams	37 grams	24 grams	3 grams

NUTRITION NEWS: The Vanilla Bean

Vanilla beans contain the B vitamins niacin, riboflavin, thiamin, and B_6. Vanilla also has trace amounts of calcium, magnesium, potassium, iron, zinc, and manganese. So, while it may seem to contain only negligible nutrition, adding vanilla to high-nutrient smoothies and juices is a great way to boost its overall nutrition score.

Mooo-Vin Milkshakes

*When kids are hoping for a banana split, this milkshake
will do the trick. With bananas, real vanilla, and a
cherry on top, this dessert hits the spot.*

FOUR 1-CUP SERVINGS

1 cup spinach

2 cups cherries, pitted

1 banana, peeled

Pulp of 1½ vanilla beans
   or 1½ teaspoons
   vanilla extract

2 cups vanilla kefir

1 cup ice

1 Place spinach, cherries, banana, vanilla bean
(or vanilla extract), and vanilla kefir in a
blender, and blend on high for 30 seconds.

2 Continue to blend while adding 1 cup ice until
smoothie is the desired consistency.

CALORIES	FAT	PROTEIN	SODIUM	CARBOHYDRATES	SUGARS	FIBER
145	1 gram	8 grams	101 milligrams	29 grams	23 grams	3 grams

MAKE IT FUN: Cherry Soda

Freeze some cherries for this smoothie, and then freeze some extra for a cherry
soda. Frozen cherries can be dropped straight into a glass of sparkling water. As
the cherries defrost into the water, they flavor up the water and turn it pink. Kids
will enjoy having this soda to drink, and you'll be glad they aren't ingesting 74
grams of sugar as with regular sodas.

Cocoa-Nutty Smoothie

*Finish off your healthy supper with this chocolate smoothie.
You won't need to nag your kids about finishing their dinnertime
vegetables, because you can add the veggies to dessert instead.*

FOUR 1-CUP SERVINGS

1 cup spinach

2 tablespoons carob
  powder

3 bananas, peeled

2 cups almond milk

1 cup ice

1 Place spinach, carob powder, bananas, and 1
cup almond milk in a blender, and blend until
smooth.

2 Add remaining 1 cup almond milk and the ice,
and blend until desired consistency is reached.

CALORIES	FAT	PROTEIN	SODIUM	CARBOHYDRATES	SUGARS	FIBER
153	2 grams	5 grams	70 milligrams	31 grams	17 grams	4 grams

GREEN TIP: Washing Your Smoothie Dishes

Washing dishes by hand actually uses more water than running an energy efficient dishwasher! However, you can be even more environmentally conscious by adding a few extra steps to your dishwashing routine. First, run the dishwasher when it is full. Running small loads more often is a huge energy drain. Second, turn down the heat. It isn't necessary to have the heat as hot as it is programmed to be. Third, turn off the dry cycle. Take the dishes out and dry with a dishtowel, or let them air dry. Drying and putting away the dishes out of the dishwasher is a great task for your kids to undertake.

The Tortoise and the Pear

Traditional desserts leave kids hyper and unable to go to sleep. Sweet treats from a natural source like fruit give kids just enough energy to make it until bedtime, without letting them get hyper.

FOUR 1-CUP SERVINGS

1 cup spinach
2 pears, cored and
    peeled
1 cup cherries, pitted
1 banana, peeled
2 cups almond milk

1 Place spinach, pears, cherries, banana, and 1 cup almond milk in a blender, and blend until smooth.

2 Add remaining 1 cup almond milk, and blend until desired texture is achieved.

CALORIES	FAT	PROTEIN	SODIUM	CARBOHYDRATES	SUGARS	FIBER
135	2 grams	5 grams	68 milligrams	25 grams	16 grams	4 grams

NUTRITION NEWS: Spinach

Packed with vitamin A, vitamin K, manganese, and folate, spinach is definitely known to be a superfood. But spinach's nutrition profile doesn't stop there. Spinach also contains fiber for good digestion, calcium for strong bones, antioxidants for halting cell damage, vitamin A for promoting vision health, vitamin B for energy, omega-3s for anti-inflammatory help, plus selenium for heart health. You may ask yourself, "Is there anything spinach doesn't have?" I'd tell you, "No, spinach has got it all."

Ginger Apple Snap

*Ending a meal with dessert is a habit for most Americans.
There is nothing wrong with keeping this behavior alive when
your dessert is as healthy as your meal. This apple-ginger
smoothie fits the craving for any after-dinner dessert.*

FOUR 1-CUP SERVINGS

1 cup romaine lettuce
2 apples, cored and
 peeled
½" gingerroot, peeled
½ cup plain Greek-
 style yogurt
1 cup ice

1 Place romaine, apples, gingerroot, and yogurt
in a blender, and mix until well combined.

2 Add the ice, and blend until smoothie is the
desired consistency.

CALORIES	FAT	PROTEIN	SODIUM	CARBOHYDRATES	SUGARS	FIBER
60	0 grams	3 grams	13 milligrams	12 grams	9 grams	1 gram

TIME SAVER TIP: Storing Ice

To save time, have homemade ice always ready for smoothies and juices in a
pinch. If your fridge has an automatic ice maker, be sure the ice chute is clean
and free of obstruction. Also, check each time you use ice to make sure the ice-
maker lever is in the "on" position. Without an ice maker, keep two or three
ice trays filled and in the freezer. When one tray is frozen, dump the ice into a
freezer-safe bag and store in the freezer. You can refill the tray, to be used after
the bag is empty.

Neptune's Nutty Spoon

Your kids aren't going to miss peanut butter and chocolate candy bars when they get to drink this almond-and-chocolate smoothie. Serve this one on Halloween night before they get their bags full of candy, and they won't be tempted to eat it all before they get home.

FOUR 1-CUP SERVINGS

¼ cup almonds
1 cup vanilla almond milk
2 tablespoons cocoa
  powder
1 cup watercress
1 banana, peeled
1 tablespoon agave
  nectar

1 Combine almonds and vanilla milk in a blender, and blend until almonds are smooth.

2 Add cocoa powder, watercress, banana, and agave, and blend until smoothie is desired consistency, about 60–90 seconds.

CALORIES	FAT	PROTEIN	SODIUM	CARBOHYDRATES	SUGARS	FIBER
116	4 grams	4 grams	35 milligrams	18 grams	11 grams	3 grams

NUTRITION NEWS: Cocoa

Cocoa has been shown in many studies to be filled with antioxidants and nutrients. The antioxidants in chocolate contribute to healthy skin, plus chocolate can increase insulin sensitivity, suppress cancer growth, improve memory, improve heart health, and help stop diarrhea. With all these benefits, cocoa can truly be called a superfood. When looking for cocoa to use in smoothies and baked goods, check the ingredient label. It's easy to find cocoa that contains 100 percent of the cocoa bean without fillers, fats, sugars, preservatives, or any other added ingredient.

Planet Mars Mango Mash Up

Kids are often the target of marketing for all the new energy drinks on the store shelves. Kids can get the energy they crave without the afternoon crash when they drink smoothies like this one, full of fruit sugar, B vitamins, and good carbs.

FOUR 1-CUP SERVINGS

1 cup iceberg lettuce

2 mangoes, peeled and
    pit removed

1 banana

2 cups orange juice

1 Combine lettuce, mangoes, banana, and 1 cup juice in a blender, and blend until smooth.

2 Continue to blend while adding remaining juice until desired consistency is reached.

CALORIES	FAT	PROTEIN	SODIUM	CARBOHYDRATES	SUGARS	FIBER
156	1 gram	2 grams	6 milligrams	39 grams	30 grams	3 grams

DIY: Bagged Salads

Paying twice as much for salads that are washed and chopped for you isn't always necessary. On shopping day, commit to washing and chopping your own greens, then bagging them for the days you'll use it. Use one bag of chopped greens for smoothies and for juices, one for salads, and a third for topping veggie wraps or sandwiches. Wrap the greens in a damp paper towel to store in the fridge, and don't place next to gas-emitting fruits like apples, bananas, or pears.

The Three Little Pears

Choosing juicy pears for this smoothie will make it stand out from all the rest. If using canned pears, use the pear juice to replace the water for extra flavor.

FOUR 1-CUP SERVINGS

1 cup spinach
3 pears, peeled and
    cored
1 banana, peeled
1 cup water

1 Take spinach, pears, banana, and ½ cup water, and place in blender. Blend for 30 seconds, pushing the food down onto the blades with a damper.

2 Add remaining water, and blend until smoothie is desired consistency.

CALORIES	FAT	PROTEIN	SODIUM	CARBOHYDRATES	SUGARS	FIBER
54	0 grams	1 gram	6 milligrams	14 grams	8 grams	3 grams

TIME SAVER TIP: Canned Fruit

Pears aren't available year-round, but canned pears are a great alternative. Look for pears packed in their own juice instead of heavy syrup or artificial sugars. For an even healthier step, look for pears that are preserved in glass jars, rather than aluminum cans, where possible.

Cherry Tales

Serve this pink smoothie at your next princess party. The party guests won't be disappointed by the amazing flavor and sweetness. Just make sure they drink them outside, unless your flooring cleans up easily!

FOUR 1-CUP SERVINGS

2 pears, cored
1 banana
1 cup cherries, pitted
½ vanilla bean pulp or 1 teaspoon vanilla extract
1 tablespoon honey
2 cups almond milk

1 Take pears, banana, cherries, vanilla bean (or vanilla extract), honey, and 1 cup almond milk, and place in a blender. Blend on high for 30 seconds.

2 Remove lid, push all unblended food down onto the blender blades, then add the remaining 1 cup almond milk.

3 Blend until smoothie is desired consistency.

CALORIES	FAT	PROTEIN	SODIUM	CARBOHYDRATES	SUGARS	FIBER
149	2 grams	5 grams	62 milligrams	29 grams	21 grams	4 grams

DIY: Cherry Pitting

Turn on the music, gather the children, put out a bowl of cherries, and start pitting. This fun activity is actually a joy for kids and parents to do together. After cherries are pitted, they can be frozen for smoothies, eaten right away, or even used in baked goods. With the pits intact, cherries are difficult to use for anything. Hold a cherry in one hand and puncture one end with a toothpick or small stick (like a manicure stick). Scrape your toothpick around the edges of the pit, and pop it out. This can be a juicy mess, so make sure you have plenty of napkins nearby.

Follow the Lemon Brick Road

*Reward your kids for working hard with this dessert smoothie.
Saturday chores won't seem so bad when the kids know it will be
followed up with this pear, banana, and lemon combo!*

FOUR 1-CUP SERVINGS

2 cups romaine lettuce
4 pears, cored
1 banana, peeled
4 tablespoons lemon
   juice
1 tablespoon honey
1 cup water

1 Place romaine, pears, banana, lemon juice, honey, and ½ cup water in a blender, and blend for 30 seconds.

2 Stir mixture, and add remaining water. Blend until smoothie is desired consistency.

CALORIES	FAT	PROTEIN	SODIUM	CARBOHYDRATES	SUGARS	FIBER
84	0 grams	1 gram	6 milligrams	22 grams	15 grams	4 grams

MAKE IT FUN: Healthy Parties

Gone are the days when a birthday party meant pizza and a movie. Take the kids roller skating, sledding, swimming, or hiking, or spend the day at the lake. Active parties are more fun because the kids can socialize and play together. Make sure the kids are well hydrated, and bring along this smoothie when they are showing signs of getting worn out. You'll send the birthday kids' home to their parents ready to crash rather than jumping off the couches.

Marvelous Melon-Cholly

Treat your kids to a midday dessert. There is no reason to wait until after dinner when this smoothie will give them a nutritious midafternoon boost. The beta-carotene, potassium, and fiber will fill them up without having them crash.

FOUR 1-CUP SERVINGS

1 cup iceberg lettuce
½ cantaloupe, rind and seeds removed
1 apple, peeled and cored
1 banana, peeled
¼" gingerroot, peeled
1 cup apple juice

1 Take lettuce, cantaloupe, apple, banana, ginger, and apple juice, and place in blender. Blend for 30 seconds.

2 Continue to blend until smoothie reaches desired consistency.

CALORIES	FAT	PROTEIN	SODIUM	CARBOHYDRATES	SUGARS	FIBER
101	0 grams	1 gram	15 milligrams	25 grams	19 grams	2 grams

TIME SAVER TIP: Party Planning

When planning the shopping list for a party, don't forget to also plan your party prep agenda. If serving fresh smoothies for the party, assemble, chop, and wash all ingredients so they are ready to be thrown into the blender as soon as guests are thirsty. The cantaloupe can be cut, cubed, and put into a bowl. The apples can be cored and peeled, and the ginger grated. Once kids are ready to eat, simply toss in and serve. It shouldn't take more than 90 seconds to get a smoothie into their hands.

Berry Potter-Melon

Watermelon juice, first sticking to little hands, and eventually sticking to your floor and shoes, can be such a mess. Blend up watermelon this summer for your next picnic party, serve outside in cups with straws, and sticky shoes will be a thing of the past.

FOUR 1-CUP SERVINGS

2 cups watermelon

1 cup raspberries

1 cup pineapple, peeled and cored

1 cup vanilla yogurt

1 Take watermelon, raspberries, pineapple, and yogurt, and place in a blender. Blend for 30 seconds, or until smooth.

2 Serve.

CALORIES	FAT	PROTEIN	SODIUM	CARBOHYDRATES	SUGARS	FIBER
111	1 gram	4 grams	42 milligrams	23 grams	19 grams	3 grams

MAKE IT FUN: Watermelon Shapes

Watermelon is an easy fruit to be creative with. Slice watermelon about 1" thick and remove the rind. Using cookie cutters, cut into watermelon to create shapes. Place shapes on skewers if they are small, or stack on a plate for a snack. Watermelon shapes can be decorated even further with some fresh basil, mint, or even sliced almonds.

Luscious Lemon

This citrus lemon slushy reminds me of a drink that we get at the fair. The fair drink, however, doesn't include any real lemon at all! It includes sugar, ice, and some artificial flavoring. Party guests will enjoy the real thing and be asking for more.

FOUR 1-CUP SERVINGS

2 lemons, peeled
2 tablespoons honey
2 cups pineapple juice
2 cups ice

1 Take lemons, honey, and pineapple juice, and place in a blender. Blend until smooth.

2 Add ice, and blend until slushy.

CALORIES	FAT	PROTEIN	SODIUM	CARBOHYDRATES	SUGARS	FIBER
107	0 grams	1 gram	4 milligrams	28 grams	22 grams	1 gram

MAKE IT FUN: Citrus-Themed Party

There are so many fun things you can do with a citrus-themed party, beyond serving a citrus smoothie. Slice oranges, lemons, and limes and fill a vase with the sliced fruit for a centerpiece. Have party décor like balloons and crepe paper in yellow and orange colors. Use a bowl of whole cloves and an orange, then have the kids puncture the orange with their cloves for their own party favor to take home. Have a blind taste-test game, and use pineapple, lemon, oranges, or grapefruit and have the kids guess which flavor they taste. Of course, follow the party with a tangy citrus lemon drink, and the kids will enjoy every minute.

Lemon Sparkleberry

Eight ounces of your typical lemon-lime soda served at birthday parties contains a whopping 25 grams of sugar! When you add the cake and ice cream, kids will have consumed more sugar than they need in a whole week. This lemon-lime soda has all the party pizzazz of the real thing without the 25 grams of sugar, of which half will likely end up spilled on your freshly shampooed carpet anyway.

FOUR 1-CUP SERVINGS

3 lemons, including the rind

3 limes, including the rind

4 cups sparkling water

1 Cut lemons and limes to fit in juicer.

2 Juice the lemons and limes, and pour equally into 4 glasses.

3 Top off with 1 cup of sparkling water in each glass.

CALORIES	FAT	PROTEIN	SODIUM	CARBOHYDRATES	SUGARS	FIBER
27	0 grams	1 gram	9 milligrams	9 grams	2 grams	3 grams

MAKE IT FUN: Healthy Parties

Replacing traditional party food with healthier fare may be easier than you think. Most kids come for the party, games, and friends. But the food can be healthy, and also be part of the fun. Fruit pizzas, fruit salad served in ice cream cones, fruit juice popsicles, frozen smoothies made into ice cream, air-popped popcorn, and baked potato chips can all be part of the party.

Frozen Apple Pie

The jump from commercial apple cider to this delicious drink will be an easy shift for your kids. They will think it's the same drink, but you'll know it's fresher and has more vitamins than apple juice that has been sitting on a store shelf.

TWO 1-CUP SERVINGS

4 Granny Smith apples
1 teaspoon cinnamon

1 Cut apples in half to fit in the juicer.

2 After juicing, mix in the cinnamon thoroughly, until dissolved.

CALORIES	FAT	PROTEIN	SODIUM	CARBOHYDRATES	SUGARS	FIBER
154	0 grams	1 gram	0 milligrams	41 grams	32 grams	4 grams

NUTRITION NEWS: *Antioxidant of Power*

Of all the culinary spices on the market today, cinnamon actually has the highest level of antioxidants. In fact, one teaspoon of cinnamon has as many antioxidants as a full cup of pomegranate juice. These antioxidants in cinnamon have been shown to regulate blood sugar and minimize inflammation. Cinnamon also contains calcium, manganese, fiber, and iron. You can incorporate cinnamon into many juices and smoothies.

Kiwi Fuzz Pop

A fruit soda actually made with fruit seems like a blast from the past. Today's fruit-flavored soda, like orange soda or fruit punch, has zero fruit. This fruit soda is mostly fruit and still fizzy.

FOUR ½-CUP SERVINGS

2 red apples
3 kiwis, peeled
1 cup sparkling water

1 Juice apples and kiwi.

2 Mix together juice from apple and kiwis, and divide into four glasses.

3 Pour ¼ cup sparkling water over juice in each cup, and stir.

CALORIES	FAT	PROTEIN	SODIUM	CARBOHYDRATES	SUGARS	FIBER
73	0 grams	1 gram	3 milligrams	19 grams	8 grams	3 grams

MAKE IT FUN: Party Drink Ideas

Change any fruit juice into a party drink with the simple addition of sparkling water. Add fun touches to the kids' cups such as mini drink umbrellas, swirled paper straws, strawberries suspended in ice cubes, frozen cherries, sliced lemons, star fruit on the end of a skewer, or even a scoop of ice cream in the glass. Use markers and stickers to decorate white paper, wrap the decorative paper around each cup, and add each child's name.

Kiwinky Drinky

High in fiber, this dessert drink is a great follow-up to party fare that may be less than healthy. Get that party cake moving quickly through digestion by following it with this juice, and your kids won't feel sick after the big day.

TWO ½-CUP SERVINGS

2 red apples, cut in half
3 kiwis, peeled

1 Push apples and kiwis into a juicer, and run through until completely juiced.

2 Collect juice from both fruits through collection spout, and stir.

CALORIES	FAT	PROTEIN	SODIUM	CARBOHYDRATES	SUGARS	FIBER
73	0 grams	1 gram	3 milligrams	19 grams	8 grams	3 grams

PICKY EATER: Hiding Juices

Parents have been puréeing fruits and vegetables to incorporate into baked goods and other popular foods for decades now. The same concept can also be applied to juices. Bake cakes for birthday parties and replace the water in the cake mix directions with homemade juices. Use kiwi juice like this one in a strawberry cake mix. Use lemon and apple juice in a yellow cake mix. Experiment with your own flavors and add some nutrients with the homemade juices to an otherwise nutrient-depleted party food.

Super Melon Man

THREE ½-CUP SERVINGS

1 cup watermelon, rind removed

1 cup cantaloupe, rind removed

1 orange, peeled

1 Juice all three fruits until they have all been processed.

2 Collect all juice into one container, and stir to mix fruit juices together.

CALORIES	FAT	PROTEIN	SODIUM	CARBOHYDRATES	SUGARS	FIBER
53	0 grams	1 gram	9 milligrams	13 grams	11 grams	2 grams

NUTRITION NEWS: Watermelon

Since every bite of watermelon is mostly water, you wouldn't think it could be so packed with nutrients. The fact is watermelon is full of lycopene, an antioxidant that may be responsible for slowing cancer growth and aging. Watermelon is also full of vitamin C, potassium, and vitamin A. It keeps kids hydrated while at the same time giving them energy and much-needed nutrients. What's even better is the watermelon flesh is encased in such a thick rind that we don't need to worry about the part we eat being saturated with pesticides. A quick rinsing of the watermelon rind is all you need to get off any dirt it may have encountered in growing. Watermelon is an excellent snack for kids to eat, drink, and enjoy all summer long.

Blue-nana Juice

The rich color in this blueberry juice gives away the fact that it is packed with the dark blue phytonutrient, anthocyanin. Although you would assume a sweet drink like this would raise blood sugar, anthocyanins have the opposite effect and can actually reduce the risk of diabetes.

THREE ½-CUP SERVINGS

2 cups blueberries
1 banana, peeled

1 Place blueberries and banana in a juicer, and turn the juicer on.

2 Collect the juice in one cup, and stir before serving.

CALORIES	FAT	PROTEIN	SODIUM	CARBOHYDRATES	SUGARS	FIBER
126	1 gram	2 grams	9 milligrams	27 grams	14 grams	5 grams

NUTRITION NEWS: Blueberries

Blueberries have earned their superfood status! They are packed with multiple different phytonutrients, including anthocyanins, hydroxycinnamic acids, hydroxybenzoic acids, flavonols, and more. Each has the ability to scavenge free radicals, helping our kids to fight inflammation, fight infections, regulate blood sugar, improve memory, support eye health, and even prevent cancer. With a superfood like this one, it's surprising pharmacists aren't bottling it up already to treat patients with! So drink some blueberry-banana juice and reap the benefits!

Sweet Pink Melon Drink

TWO ½-CUP SERVINGS

1 cup watermelon, rind
   removed
1 lime, peeled

1 First juice the watermelon, then the lime.

2 Collect juices from both fruits into one cup,
   and stir before serving.

CALORIES	FAT	PROTEIN	SODIUM	CARBOHYDRATES	SUGARS	FIBER
33	0 grams	1 gram	1 milligram	9 grams	5 grams	1 gram

TIME SAVER TIP:
Memorize Common Kitchen Conversions

Save time in the kitchen by hanging a conversion chart in your pantry or memorize certain conversions. There are certain conversions we use more than others. To save time, memorize the common ones.

CONVERSIONS	
MEASURE	**SAME AS**
3 teaspoons	1 tablespoon
¼ cup	4 tablespoons
1 cup	8 ounces
1 pint	2 cups
4 cups	1 quart
1 gallon	4 quarts
16 ounces	1 pound

Green Garden Party Punch

No drink served at a party can stand a nutritional chance against this vitamin-packed party punch. Full of vegetable greens and herbs, this drink will have kids talking about it long after the balloons have popped.

FOUR 1-CUP SERVINGS

1 bunch spinach
1 cucumber, peeled
½ bunch celery, including the leaves
1 bunch parsley
½" piece fresh gingerroot
2 green apples, cored
½ lime, peeled
½ lemon, peeled

1 Juice each fruit or vegetable one at a time, collecting juice extract into one large bowl.

2 Stir juices together to combine.

CALORIES	FAT	PROTEIN	SODIUM	CARBOHYDRATES	SUGARS	FIBER
78	1 gram	3 grams	75 milligrams	18 grams	10 grams	4 grams

NUTRITION NEWS: Parsley

Adding parsley to this vegetable-based drink isn't just for bigger flavor! Two tablespoons of parsley provide your kids with over 150 percent of the recommended daily amount for vitamin K. Parsley is also a good source of vitamin A, folate, and vitamin C. The nutrients in parsley have been shown to protect the heart, reduce arthritis symptoms, and repair unhealthy cells that contribute to diabetes and asthma.

Charming Cherry Melon

Scoop melon balls out of a watermelon and cantaloupe. Then let the melon balls float on top of this juice, served in a punch bowl. Cherries are a superfood because they have loads of antioxidants whether you eat them fresh, juiced, dried, or frozen!

TWO ½-CUP SERVINGS

1 cup watermelon, rind removed
1 cup cherries, pitted
½ lime, peeled

1 Juice the watermelon, cherries, and lime into one container.

2 Stir juices together, and top with melon balls.

CALORIES	FAT	PROTEIN	SODIUM	CARBOHYDRATES	SUGARS	FIBER
76	0 grams	1 gram	1 milligram	20 grams	15 grams	2 grams

MAKE IT FUN: Skewered Melons

Garnish individual drinks with skewered frozen melon balls. With a melon baller, scoop out the flesh of honeydew melons, cantaloupe, and even watermelon. Spread out the balls of melon on a parchment-lined baking sheet. Put in the freezer for an hour or longer. When melon is mostly frozen, push them onto a skewer in a colorful pattern. Use the melon skewer in individual cups for decorating. Drink the juice and then eat the melon.

Orange Lemonade Lift-Off

Simple and sweet, this orange-and-lemon drink only needs two ingredients. Serve this juice for a refreshing midafternoon pick-me-up and it is sure to wake up tired tots.

TWO ½-CUP SERVINGS

3 oranges, peeled
1 lemon, peeled

1 Juice the orange and the lemon together.

2 Stir before serving.

CALORIES	FAT	PROTEIN	SODIUM	CARBOHYDRATES	SUGARS	FIBER
101	0 grams	2 grams	0 milligrams	25 grams	19 grams	6 grams

GREEN TIP: Zesting Lemons and Limes

No need to waste the peel of your delicious citrus fruits. Lemon, orange, or lime zest is made by using the small holes on a grater and carefully grating off the outermost portion of the fruit. Do not grate down to the white membrane because it tastes bitter. Make sure the fruit is cleaned and dried well, even if you are purchasing organic fruit. Use the zest to top juices or smoothies and in pastries, pancakes, breads, pies, meat marinades, salads, or anything that needs a little zest added to it.

Razzle Dazzle Berry

Turn simple berry juice into a party drink with a dollop of whipped topping and sprinkles. Give kids their own cups to decorate and keep for the refills they'll be asking for.

TWO ½-CUP SERVINGS

2 cups strawberries, hulls intact

2 cups raspberries

1 Juice the strawberries and the raspberries together.

2 Combine the juice, and stir until well mixed.

CALORIES	FAT	PROTEIN	SODIUM	CARBOHYDRATES	SUGARS	FIBER
110	1 gram	2 grams	3 milligrams	26 grams	12 grams	11 grams

TIME SAVER TIP: Fruit Salad

Fruit salad is an easy and quick party side dish you can make without chopping or peeling. Take 1 can chopped pineapple pieces, 1 basket raspberries, 1 vine of grapes (pluck them from the vine), 1 cup blueberries, and 1 can drained mandarin oranges. A dump-and-go salad like this tastes fresh, it's easy, and it's well-received by kids.

Monkey's Banana Juice

Kick back for family movie night with this juice, some popcorn, and some candied nuts. The apples and blackberries are sweet and yummy, and the lemon delivers some thirst-quenching action.

THREE ½-CUP SERVINGS

2 Granny Smith apples
2 cups blackberries
1 lemon, peeled
1 banana, peeled

1 Juice the apples, blackberries, lemon, and then the banana in a single pitcher.

2 Stir together until the juices are well blended.

CALORIES	FAT	PROTEIN	SODIUM	CARBOHYDRATES	SUGARS	FIBER
133	0 grams	2 grams	2 milligrams	33 grams	2 grams	8 grams

GREEN TIP: Lemons for Cleaning

Juice one of your lemons for this drink, and save the rest for some spring green cleaning. Lemons are great for kid-friendly cleaning because they are natural and nontoxic. Let your kids use a lemon to clean the microwave. Cut a lemon in half, place in a bowl of water, and cook the water in a microwave for several minutes. Take the lemon water out, and your caked-on spills will wipe right up. Put lemon peels in your garbage disposal, and turn it on with running water. This cleans and deodorizes your disposal. Take half a lemon, dip it in baking soda, and use it to polish a stainless steel sink. Having extra lemons on hand is always a smart thing to do.

Planet of the Grapes

*Filled with delicious, vine-ripened fruits, this sweet dessert juice is
the perfect replacement for fruit punch. Serve it with popcorn at your
next movie party for the ultimate post-popcorn thirst quencher.*

TWO ½-CUP SERVINGS

1 cup red grapes
1 red apple, cored
5 cherries, pitted
½ lemon, peeled

1 Combine grapes, apple, cherries, and lemon in
a juicer, and juice.

2 Collect the juice into one container, and stir
before serving.

CALORIES	FAT	PROTEIN	SODIUM	CARBOHYDRATES	SUGARS	FIBER
107	0 grams	1 gram	2 milligrams	29 grams	23 grams	3 grams

MAKE IT FUN: Icy Juices

After making this juice, put any leftovers in the freezer for several hours. When
your kids are ready to enjoy, take all the frozen juice and put in a blender. Blend
for a few seconds until the ice is sufficiently chopped and the juice is the consistency of an "icy." Scoop the juice into cups or bowls and serve with a spoon.
This smooth, sorbet-tasting juice is the perfect dessert for hot summer days!

Purple Pomegranate Punch

The dark, delicious purple in this pomegranate juice is fun for kids whose favorite color is purple. Kids can enjoy the benefits of pomegranate without having to eat the actual pomegranate.

TWO ½-CUP SERVINGS

2 pomegranates, seeded

2 red apples, cored

1 Feed pomegranate seeds through a juicer.

2 Push the apples through the juicer, and collect in a single container with the pomegranate juice.

3 Stir the juices from the two fruits until well combined.

CALORIES	FAT	PROTEIN	SODIUM	CARBOHYDRATES	SUGARS	FIBER
311	4 grams	5 grams	8 milligrams	73 grams	55 grams	13 grams

GREEN TIP: Buy Local Produce

The buzz in the green world is to buy local food, but where do you start? There are food co-ops, visiting farmers, farmers' markets, CSA's, roadside stands, buying clubs, and local grocery stores that carry local produce. To find places in your area to purchase local food, try a comprehensive mapping site that can give you options within a certain range of your home. An easy one to use can be found at *http://www.eatwellguide.org/*. Categorize by farmers who will sell to you, or find addresses of local farmers' markets. Finding where local food is being sold has never been easier.

Blackberry Boombah

Sweet blackberries and apples combined to make this delicious, heart healthy juice. Similar combinations are sold on the market that cost more and contain less juice. Make it yourself for that same familiar taste, without the familiar cost.

TWO ½-CUP SERVINGS

2 red Gala apples, cored
4 cups blackberries
1 lemon, peeled

1 Juice the apples, blackberries, and lemon into a single container or cup.

2 Stir thoroughly, and store in refrigerator until well chilled.

CALORIES	FAT	PROTEIN	SODIUM	CARBOHYDRATES	SUGARS	FIBER
419	3 grams	10 grams	7 milligrams	101 grams	62 grams	36 grams

TIME SAVER TIP: Frozen Berries

Fresh blackberries are only available for a limited time. The rest of the year, the price tag is high because they have to be shipped across the country. Frozen berries are a great alternative for families who love this juice. Frozen berries save time because you can always have berries available in the freezer anytime you wish to have this juice. Simply thaw berries in the refrigerator a few hours to a full day before you are ready to make this juice. Then, push the berries through your juicer, just as you would do if the berries were fresh. The taste is just as delicious. Make sure you purchase frozen berries with no sugar packed or added, or freeze your own.

Kiwi Crush

Rich in vitamins and minerals, kiwis are a great part of a child's diet. With more vitamin C than an orange and more potassium than bananas, kiwi is a great source of nutrients when the other fruits aren't in season.

TWO ½-CUP SERVINGS

2 pears
2 kiwis, peeled
½ lemon, peeled

1 Juice the pears, kiwis, and lemon into a single container.

2 Stir juices together and chill until ready to drink. Stir again before serving.

CALORIES	FAT	PROTEIN	SODIUM	CARBOHYDRATES	SUGARS	FIBER
86	1 gram	1 gram	4 milligrams	22 grams	6 grams	6 grams

GREEN TIP: Storing Pears

Pears are difficult to store and transport. They bruise easily, and their fragile skin gets torn up with the slightest touch. Pears in the pantry only last from 1–4 days. Pears stored in the refrigerator can last up to 7 days. Frozen pears can last up to a year. You may store pears on the kitchen counter or in the pantry in a paper bag until ripe. Once ripe, however, move pears to a plastic bag and keep in the refrigerator. Once 7 days have passed, if you still have pears left, juice them for this drink.

Gusty Grapefruit

Juicy, tart, and tangy grapefruits make delicious juices.
When serving grapefruit juices for dessert, add a little
sweetener to help kids drink it down in one gulp!

TWO ½-CUP SERVINGS

½ **pink grapefruit, rind
removed**
½ **white grapefruit,
rind removed**
1 teaspoon honey

1 Juice both grapefruits into one cup.

2 Add the honey and stir well. Store juice in the
refrigerator until you are ready to serve.

CALORIES	FAT	PROTEIN	SODIUM	CARBOHYDRATES	SUGARS	FIBER
31	0 grams	0 grams	0 milligrams	8 grams	7 grams	1 gram

NUTRITION NEWS: Sweeteners

Many sweeteners can be used interchangeably in juices; however, some are
healthier than others. Natural sweeteners are sweeteners that are closer to
the way they are grown than commercialized or processed sweeteners. For
example, a stevia plant is going to be more natural than stevia that has been
stripped, boiled down, extracted, and packaged. Natural sweeteners that work
well in juices include blackstrap molasses, brown rice syrup, date sugar, honey,
maple syrup, agave, and stevia. The closer a sweetener is to Mother Nature, the
more nutrients it will have retained.

Orange Squirt

Broccoli has never been used in a dessert recipe before now. If you have been looking for a way to get your kids to eat their broccoli, look no further than this orange juice. The subtle hint of this superfood is overpowered by the sweet oranges.

TWO ½-CUP SERVINGS

2 oranges, peeled
1 cup broccoli, washed

1 Juice the oranges and then the broccoli into a single pitcher.

2 Stir the juices together well before serving.

CALORIES	FAT	PROTEIN	SODIUM	CARBOHYDRATES	SUGARS	FIBER
77	0 grams	3 grams	15 milligrams	18 grams	13 grams	4 grams

MAKE IT FUN: Family Campout

Take this juice outside and start a tradition with your kids. Every summer, consider a family campout in the backyard. You'll have the convenience of your home bathroom a few steps away, yet you can enjoy the crisp, cool air and the beautiful nighttime stars. Often, kids aren't awake late enough in the summer to observe the night sky, but when you sleep outside together, they can't help but wait until it's dark to fall asleep. This family tradition will be a favorite as they grow up. They'll remember the smells, the taste of the juices, and the safety of their family sleeping right next to them.

Alice the Cantaloupe

Vanilla and honey in this juice takes the flavor beyond traditional homemade juices. The honey doubles as a sweetener as well as a throat soother. Kids a little under the weather don't need to be left out of all the fun!

TWO ½-CUP SERVINGS

½ cantaloupe, rind removed
1 lime, peeled
1 tablespoon honey
1 teaspoon pure vanilla extract

1 Push cantaloupe and lime through the spout of a juicer, and juice.

2 Collect the juice in a single container, and stir.

3 Add vanilla and honey to the juice, and stir well.

CALORIES	FAT	PROTEIN	SODIUM	CARBOHYDRATES	SUGARS	FIBER
95	0 grams	1 gram	23 milligrams	24 grams	20 grams	2 grams

DIY: Making Vanilla Extract

Homemade vanilla extract is not only tastier and less expensive than commercial varieties, but it's actually fun for the kids to make. For best results, traditional homemade vanilla is made by using 2 or 3 vanilla beans and a cup of vodka. You can make it without the alcohol, however. Scrape the seeds from 2 vanilla beans into a tall jar. Throw away the outer shell of the bean, only preserving the meat inside. Add 12 ounces of glycerin and 4 ounces of warm water. Store in a cool, dark place for about one month. Shake often and have your kids notice the color changes in the jar over the month. After one month, your vanilla is ready to use in this juice, as well as in baking. Your homemade vanilla will last as long as you want it to. In fact, the longer you keep it, the better it will taste.

Jungle Ginger Juice

At your next baby shower or family party, fill a punch bowl with this jungle juice. Then, scoop some sorbet, soda, and frozen raspberries into the punch bowl as well. Serve with a large ladle into cups.

TWO ½-CUP SERVINGS

1 pint blackberries
1 pint raspberries
½ lemon, peeled
¼" slice gingerroot, peeled

1 Juice the blackberries, raspberries, lemon, and ginger into one large punch bowl.

2 Stir juices together until well combined.

CALORIES	FAT	PROTEIN	SODIUM	CARBOHYDRATES	SUGARS	FIBER
132	2 grams	4 grams	3 milligrams	30 grams	13 grams	16 grams

NUTRITION NEWS: Antioxidants

You hear often that dark berries like these are full of antioxidants. But what are antioxidants? Antioxidants are a broad category of nutrients that have the ability to slow oxidative damage to cells caused by free radicals. These chemically active free radicals steal electrons, making cells unstable. Antioxidants donate electrons to stabilize the cells. Unstable, damaged cells are believed to be the cause of many chronic diseases, aging, and inflammation. So, eating foods full of antioxidants help our bodies to prevent disease and slow aging.

Fresh and Sweet, Banana Treat

*A squirt of lemon in this apple-banana drink keeps it
fresh and tasty. Save this juice for the next slumber party,
if you can make enough for all your thirsty little guests.*

TWO ½-CUP SERVINGS

**3 Granny Smith apples,
cored**

1 lemon, peeled

1 banana, peeled

1 Juice the apples, lemon, and banana, pushing
each fruit through the juicer one at a time.

2 Collect the juice into a single pitcher, and stir
when you are ready to serve.

CALORIES	FAT	PROTEIN	SODIUM	CARBOHYDRATES	SUGARS	FIBER
177	1 gram	2 grams	1 milligram	47 grams	32 grams	5 grams

MAKE IT FUN: Party Punch

Turn this simple juice into a party treat by adding a smidge of all-fruit jam! Use
½ cup raspberry jam for every 4 cups of apple-banana juice. Slowly whisk the
jam into the juice until it is well combined. Keep all the party punch in a large
punch bowl, fill with ice, and serve using a ladle. While this juice is super sweet,
there is no added sugar, chemicals, or bad stuff.

Goo Goo Grape

Grape juice with a splash of pear is delicious during family game night. Serve a bowl of grapes to snack on and some juice to top it off, and your kids will never want game night to end.

TWO ½-CUP SERVINGS

2 pears

1 cup red grapes

1 Juice the pears and the grapes, and collect into a single cup or pitcher.

2 Stir juices around until the two juices are well integrated.

CALORIES	FAT	PROTEIN	SODIUM	CARBOHYDRATES	SUGARS	FIBER
87	0 grams	1 gram	2 milligrams	23 grams	18 grams	4 grams

TIME SAVER TIP: Snacking on Grapes

Having a bowl of grapes for a party, halftime at a soccer game, or just in the fridge for your kids will generally be well received. However, little hands often retrieve the entire grapevine when they only want a couple of grapes. Take a pair of kitchen shears and cut the grapevine into small segments, each branch containing ten to twelve grapes. Now when your little guests grab some grapes, they'll only take a portion big enough for personal snacking. This is a great alternative to having them grab the whole vine or trying to rip off a piece of the branch.

Freckleberry Lemon Juice

Raspberry lemonade is a popular drink at many restaurants, and it certainly will be popular with your kids. Try serving this on game night, with the family gathered around cheering on your favorite football team.

TWO ½-CUP SERVINGS

4 cups raspberries

1 lemons, peeled

1 Juice the raspberries and the lemon into a single container or pitcher.

2 Stir the juices thoroughly until well combined.

CALORIES	FAT	PROTEIN	SODIUM	CARBOHYDRATES	SUGARS	FIBER
136	2 grams	3 grams	3 milligrams	32 grams	12 grams	17 grams

MAKE IT FUN: Raspberry Fizzle

Turn this juice into dessert by making this delicious Raspberry Fizzle. First, place 1½ cups raspberry juice into a blender. Add 3 scoops raspberry sherbet into the blender. Then add ½ cup sparkling water or carbonated water. Blend completely. Pour into a glass and serve.

Index

Note: Page numbers in **bold** indicate recipe category lists.

About the Authors

Amy Roskelley has been helping families eat better and live healthier for fifteen years. After graduating with a BSc in Community Health, she worked for the health department counseling employees about losing weight, lowering blood pressure, improving cholesterol, and exercise. Amy also worked two years for a state program that introduced health policies and programs to elementary schools. Now, with three kids of her own in tow, Amy maintains a blog online at *www.superhealthykids.com*, with healthy meal plans, recipes, and ideas for parents to encourage their kids to be healthy.

Nicole Cormier, RD, LDN is a registered dietitian and owner of the nutrition counseling company Delicious Living Nutrition. She wrote *The Everything® Healthy College Cookbook* and coauthored *The Everything® Juicing Book*.